EAST meets WEST

Journey Through War & Peace
From The Mekong Delta To San Francisco Bay

VOLUME
1

EAST meets WEST

Journey by: **Khương Hữu Điểu**
Cover by: **Khương Hữu Điểu & Khánh Trường**
Layout by: **Lê Hân**
Review & Correction by: **Thái Vĩnh Khiêm & Stanley Tull**
Technique by: **Tạ Quốc Quang**
ISBN: **9781989705520**
Nhân Ảnh Publisher **2018**
Copyright @ 2018 by Dieu Khuong-Huu

Table of Contents for Volume 1

Introduction	9
PART I: The Beauty of Life in the Mekong Delta	
Chapter 1: My Early Years as a Teenager in Vietnam	17
Chapter 2: Peaceful Life along the Mekong Delta	47
Chapter 3: My Childhood Fun in the Mekong Delta	77
PART II: Learning the French Way	
Chapter 4: A Taste of Competition at Le Myre De Vilers, My Tho	103
Chapter 5: Da Lat & Lycée Yersin	117
PART III: Learning the American Way	
Chapter 6: Immersion in Lafayette College, Pennsylvania, USA	153
Chapter 7: Challenge at MIT	183
Chapter 8: Work and Fun in New York City	207
PART IV: Time to Go Home	
Chapter 9: New York – Saigon in 90 days via Pan Am	235
Chapter 10: My Saigon Life from 1958-1975	329
PART V: A Nation Governed in Time of War	
Chapter 11: ESSO – The Inside Story	363
Chapter 12: Perils of Industrialization during War Time	375
Chapter 13: Offshore Oil Exploration	393

Table of Contents for Volume 2

PART V: A Nation Governed in Time of War
(continued from Volume 1)

Chapter 14: Creation of Industrial Infrastructure in War Time — 411

Chapter 15: International Cooperation — 427

PART VI: Escape from Vietnam

Chapter 16: Saigon to the U.S — 457

Chapter 17: Refugees in Marine Camp Pendleton, California — 471

PART VII: Politics in Time of War

Chapter 18: Kissinger and the Vietnam War — 497

PART VIII: Finding a New Life

Chapter 19: Good Samaritans — 521

Chapter 20: San Francisco, Home Sweet Home — 545

PART IX: The Beauty of Life Here and Now

Chapter 21: Twenty-Two Years of Work for a Happy Retirement — 585

Chapter 22: Gastronomy and My Life — 615

Chapter 23: Retirement with Health, Happiness and Quality Life — 653

Chapter 24: Anecdotes from "Dream Team" — 683

Chapter 25: Bonds of Love Among Siblings — 777

Epilogue / Acknowledgements — 817

Appendix — 823

Introduction

By fate or by destiny my grandmother decided that I would be named "qui Dieu," the Vietnamese word for "Eagle." Little did she know how appropriate the name would be, for the eagle has come to symbolize my life - through all of my journeys and aspirations to fly above the rest and thrive in spite of the challenges that have come before me - in both the East and the West. My first flight across the Pacific was for education. My last flight across the same ocean was for survival. According to Rudyard Kipling "East is East, and West is West, and never the twain shall meet." But I have asked myself, when "East meets West, then what?" Since the melding of East and West has truly defined my life, I have chosen to tackle this question by sharing the story of my life - from my childhood in the Mekong Delta to the latter half of my life in San Francisco, where I ended up after coming to America as a refugee following the Vietnam War.

I have never written a book in my life, so why would I do so now at the ripe old age of eighty plus years? Well, when you reach this stage of your existence, there is a popular saying in Vietnam reminding you that "you have come much nearer to the bosom of the earth, and a bit farther away from heavens above," or as one would say in the west, I am close to the point of "ashes to ashes, and dust to dust." This is the time of life when all kinds of memories begin to flash back to you with increasing intensity. Very often in the evening, when sitting alone in the quiet of my back garden, all kinds of things surge into my head with a multitude of images from my distant past.

These moments of reminiscing can be extremely emotional and quite chaotic at the same time. For this reason, I have tried to put this kaleidoscope of memories, which in fact consists of my life's story, into some semblance of order. I decided to start writing down these memories in case they might not come back to me again, and the pages just piled up. This prompted me to organize them, not only in terms of time and space, but together with the thoughts, feelings and emotions that I felt along the way - all of which have helped me to become the person that I am today. I have accumulated several hundred pages of memoirs over the past few years of my retirement, so upon the insistence of many of my friends and relatives, I have chosen to share them in the form of this book.

So much for the origin of this book and its title. Beyond simply recording the events of my life, this book is, above all, dedicated to my beloved parents, to my dearest wife Marie who has stood by my side for better and for worse over the past 55 years, and to the members of my extended family as well as numerous friends in Vietnam, the US, and elsewhere in the world who may wish to know more about the story of my life.

I spent the first half of my life in tumultuous Asia, specifically Vietnam. I lived through French colonialism, the Japanese invasion followed by the return of the French expeditionary troops with more war and re-occupation until the Geneva Accords of 1954 which partitioned Vietnam at the 17th parallel thus establishing communist North Vietnam and nationalist South Vietnam. The predominant context of this first half of my life was, of course, the war in Vietnam which came to an end in 1975 but has remained a subject of endless and heated debate to this day even among the experts and pundits. The war in Vietnam must be remembered as one of the greatest collective tragedies of the 20th century, the most devastating armed conflict in the 4,000 years of Vietnam's written history, and the longest foreign war for the American people since the birth of their nation more than two hundred years ago. For me, having been exposed to both the Vietnamese and American ways of life, that dreadful war represents an enormous and violent clash of civilizations, and the terrible consequences of when "EAST meets WEST" in the land of my ancestors.

The second half of my life began in April 1975 when I arrived at Camp Pendleton, California. After the fall of Saigon in 1975, at age 44, I lost my country, my home, and my possessions - all things I held dear in my life. Stepping out of Camp Pendleton, I had to overcome the extreme hardship and challenges of a refugee with nothing to my name but $150 in traveler's checks and a handbag of old clothes. This second half of my life has encompassed 22 years of hard work, followed by almost 20 years of comfortable retirement in my adopted country.

I must thank my Creator for giving me this second chance in America and not somewhere else, for I deeply cherish the privilege of living in a country of freedom and opportunity. I had never wished to abandon, or be separated from, my native homeland but remaining in Viet Nam under the totalitarian communist regime was never an option for me and my wife, Marie. It is quite amazing that the fateful and dramatic year of 1975, which has left a deep and indelible scar, sliced my entire life story into two almost equal periods of 40 years. Both parts have been filled with mixed feelings of great joy and happiness, along with profound pain and suffering. During these two long periods of my life, I had three major encounters of "EAST meets WEST." First, during my stay in America for my education from 1952 to 1958, then back in Saigon and through the war which seemed to prove Rudyard Kipling correct, and finally from 1975 on, as a refugee in America with my laborious efforts to secure a meaningful life during which I have shown that East and West can successfully meet in America!

Introduction

As an American citizen with a hybrid Eastern and Western viewpoint, a Chinese-Vietnamese cultural background, and a combined Vietnamese, French and American education, I want to retrace my journey from my peaceful life in the Mekong Delta of the 1930's to the high tech San Francisco Bay Area of the 21st century. In 1952, long before the American intervention in Viet Nam, I left Saigon to pursue a Fulbright scholarship in the US. Over the next seven years I was fortunate to receive an excellent education from Lafayette College, then the prestigious MIT, and later from Columbia University. In 1958, I returned home to serve in the nationalist South Vietnamese government in Saigon until April 1975 when I was thankfully able to escape the violent Bolshevik-like takeover of the whole country. A new era, the "rebirth of the eagle," had started - going through the full circle of riches to rags, and from rags to riches once again.

My initial Trans-Pacific journey from the East to the West in 1952 quickly and drastically changed my life. I left an underdeveloped French colony in old Indochina and flew over the Pacific Ocean to study engineering in America, the most advanced country of the world after WWII. The trip itself was incredible for a Vietnamese youngster in the early 1950s. For me, it was my maiden flight from the shores of the Mekong Delta in Vietnam to the San Francisco Bay in America. It was also the beginning of my personal adventure of "EAST meets WEST."

My Fulbright scholarship allowed me a few days of orientation in the great city of San Francisco to prepare myself for my very first contact with life in America. After that initial clash between East and West, my journey continued smoothly to Lafayette College in Easton, Pennsylvania. In all respects, I was "thrown into the ocean to learn how to swim" instead of being gradually immersed into my new environment and the use of the English language. Being uprooted from my traditional Asian family life was, of course, a real nightmare. Homesickness, loneliness, and the language barrier were my worst enemies. Somehow, by surviving all of these challenges, I became a lot stronger and my skin became thicker. These first four years in Pennsylvania transformed my life, making me more independent and more prepared for the tough steps ahead. The next challenge was MIT, along with my head-grinding efforts to complete my graduate studies as quickly as possible and acquire the professional skills I needed before returning home.

I was determined to study very hard during my years of schooling in America, even if I had to sacrifice fun and leisure in order to succeed academically. The results were simply astonishing. I was consistently at the top of my class, even though many of my classmates were much more intelligent than I was. After graduating from MIT I spent some time working and enjoying myself in New York City. Then finally, in 1958, I made the memorable decision to return to Vietnam, with a ticket on Pan American Airways that enabled me to travel the world for 90 days en route.

Returning home was a real life" Rip van Winkle" experience for me. As soon as my parents and relatives appeared at Saigon Tân Sơn Nhứt airport to welcome me home after our long separation, I realized that my years in the US had been a period of luxury living and a safe haven from the escalating war in Viet Nam. The stark realities about my homeland hit me in full force. And so began a completely new chapter of my life in South Viet Nam. Before getting too settled, I took care of my top priorities - I got married, I bought a house, and began my career.

During my 17 years of hard work in Saigon in the government civilian sector, I did my best to contribute and serve my beloved country which was impoverished by continuous enemy infiltration and armed aggression by communist North Vietnam. In 1966, at age 35, I was the youngest ever Deputy Minister of Economy of South Vietnam, managing an $800 million civilian aid program and millions of dollars of Viet Nam's own foreign exchange. I had the chance to form a strong team of "young Turk technocrats." They created the entire necessary infrastructure for the economic development of war-torn Vietnam. In 1967, together with the Vietnamese Minister of Economy & Finance Âu Trường Thanh, I had the opportunity to visit President Johnson and his adviser Mr. Walt Rostow in the White House. Also in attendance was McGeorge Bundy, US National Security Advisor. The purpose of the meeting was to review the economic challenges in our struggling country that had been so impacted by the war.

My dream to see a peaceful and prosperous South Viet Nam never did come true. By April 1975, the situation became a nightmare, and the subsequent fall of Saigon precipitated my second journey to the U.S. - but this time with shock and surprise. The next thing I knew, my wife and I were alive and uninjured in Camp Pendleton in California where my fellow refugees elected me mayor of the camp to take care of thousands of Vietnamese families arriving day after day. From there, a new chapter of my life began, with years of hard work, stress, sweat and fun, followed by my current happy, prosperous and, most of all, healthy retirement in my adopted hometown of San Francisco. My second phase of "EAST meets WEST" is surely now reaching its final stages.

I feel lucky and gratified to be able to record these two long journeys: first from a relatively peaceful Viet Nam, and then the second from a Viet Nam that had been destroyed by war. When I first left Vietnam, it was only to pursue my education, but when I left my native country for the second time, I had the distressful feeling that this goodbye was for good. I was filled with profound sadness at the loss of freedom and democracy for the Vietnamese people, and also for the painful thought that I would never again see the land of my ancestors, and I cried...

Looking back at these memories, spanning the Pacific Ocean and over eight decades, my journey of "EAST meets WEST" has also been an inner one, which has deeply affected my heart and mind. With the amazing human capacity for evolution and adaptation, I remember gradually integrating into the American lifestyle. Little by little I was able to understand the so-called "melting pot," which has made it possible for hundreds of millions of people from different races, creeds and cultures to have succeeded in creating a society in which to live together in peace. Collectively, they have made extraordinary achievements, by way of tremendous sacrifice, sweat and tears, in all fields of human endeavors. Whether one likes it or not, the melting pot of America has proven to be a unique, but successful, experiment in the history of humankind.

After four continuous decades of living in the United States, I can say that the second half of my life was filled with great challenges. But in this land of the free, I have learned that honesty and hard work can claim its legitimate rewards for people who wish to have a decent and respectable life. For me, America is exceptional, not because it has become the richest and most powerful nation in the world, but because it has propagated its ideals of freedom and democracy to the four corners of the earth, ever since its birth as a nation in 1776. It continues to do so and is a beacon of light for oppressed people everywhere who are fighting against totalitarianism and dictatorship. Nowadays, many millions of people continue to look at America as the land of asylum, refuge and survival, as I did in 1975.

The reader will note this book contains many photos of U.S. landmark sites, which will be familiar to all Americans, and thus wonder why the need for such photos. My answer is that my book is to be translated into Vietnamese and distributed among Vietnamese readers, many of whom will not be familiar with these American landmarks.

It has been a worthwhile and exciting journey. Let me now tell you my unique and personal story of "EAST meets WEST"- My flight of the Eagle from the shores of the Mekong Delta to the San Francisco Bay.

Khương Hữu Điểu
The Golden State
2017

PART I

The Beauty of Life in the Mekong Delta

CHAPTER 1

My Early Years as a Teenager in Vietnam

The Family Founder

My Grand Mother Khương-Hữu Lương (photo 1936)
Founder of Khương-Hữu family

Though most people who know me would agree that I am a straight talker and a straight shooter, there is nothing straight about the circumstances surrounding the date, place, and parents' names on my birth certificate. I can assure you with a straight face that all those facts are plainly verifiable and known to a small circle of family members or close friends but they were kept from my knowledge for quite a long time. As a straight talker, I feel that I owe the readers some explanations. I would like to set things straight so that there is no misunderstanding about my identity.

Long before I came into this life, my paternal grandmother had decided that my father would name his children in this sequence **"Ngân, Đáng, Ngàn, Cân, Sứng, Lắm, Quí, Điểu."** This phrase, literally translated, means "Precious Bird Worth Matching Really Thousand Pound Silver." From that phrase, it was apparent that she intended for my father to have at least eight children. As my wife would later remark with a touch of humor, when my mother became pregnant for the 7th and also last time, to please her mother-in-law, she made sure that she would give birth to *twins* in order to complete the name sequence. I was lucky to be her eighth child and was given the name "Quí Điểu=Precious Bird=Eagle."

The Twins, 1931 "Precious Bird"

Thank God it was the name of a valiant, precious bird - not that of a crow or a turkey! Only an Eagle can soar. My whole adult life has been guided by that soaring image. Later I learned to "soar with the eagles, not run with the turkeys."

My birthplace: Mỹ Tho Maternity Hospital

Things so far look simple and straightforward enough. Now comes the confusing part. My father's brother number seven, "Uncle Seven," had no children. According to Vietnamese tradition, each family should have a son to carry on the family name and take care of the ancestor's altar or organize the "Đám Giỗ," or annual Memorial Service. So, my father decided to give me to him for adoption. I said it's confusing because now I had to call my father "Uncle Five" and my Uncle Seven "father."

The confusion did not stop there. Both sets of parents did not want me to know that I was adopted. My twin brother and I were born at the Mỹ Tho Provincial Maternity Hospital. Yet on the birth certificates, we were given different birth places, birth dates, and sets of parents:

Khương Hữu Điểu	**Khương Hữu Quí**
October 7, 1931	**Septembre 19, 1931**
Thiềng Đức Village	**Điều Hòa Village**
Vĩnh Long Province	**Mỹ Tho Province**
Father: Khương-Hữu Bảy	**Father: Khương-Hữu Lân**
Mother: Nguyễn thị Nhị	**Mother: Nguyễn thị Vàng**

(Vĩnh Long and Mỹ Tho are 70 Km apart!)

My grandmother and biological parents

My bio parents

My adoptive parents hereinafter referred to as my parents, 1936

Trip to Nha Trang with my parents 1940 *My father and me 1944*

"Tết" family photo on the home roof garden at 59 Quai Gallieni, Mỹ Tho, 1944
L to R: My Father, Me, Mother, Sister Six, Aunt Five, Sister Two, Brother Five & Wife, Sister Two's daughter Ho, Sister Seven

My Parents   *My father*

The parents' game plan of splitting the twins on the birth certificates seemed to work quite well because now at 86, I still cannot call my biological father "father" and my biological uncle "uncle." When I was five years old, my sisters would attempt to cajole me into calling my biological mother "mother." I just could not do it. They had to bribe me with chocolate bars or some other tempting things each time they wanted to hear me say it.

During our early years, because the twins looked so much alike, to avoid calling us by the wrong name people combined our first names and called us **"Quí-Điểu"** or "Precious Bird." I knew the truth about my situation in the family and my parent's decision about this switching process only when my brain became good enough to catch the rumor about me. My father and uncle lived and worked together as a team and I, therefore, spent a lot of time among my siblings. Ah! The mysterious ways of the East!

In traditional Vietnamese families, children of younger brothers occupy lower ranks than those of elder ones. That's the underdog lot, the first cross I had to bear! Furthermore, children of richer brothers have higher status than those of poorer ones. My biological father, Uncle Five was the best and richest entrepreneur in the family. As a result, he was wealthy enough to bail out all the other brothers in need including my father. Another unwanted load that was mine to shoulder! Nevertheless, the silver lining to all this was that it rendered me better equipped or prepared to deal with adversities in my later years.

Every Tết "Vietnamese lunar New Year" my bio parents, in traditional gown, had a group photo with children and grandchildren.

From left to right:
Standing in the back row: my sister Seven, myself, my father, sister Six, sister Four, my twin, and my mother. The kids in front were children from sister Two and sister Six.

This photo was taken at my father's rice mill property and fruit plantation, Mỹ Tho 1948:

Building KHƯƠNG HỮU Mỹ Tho

Lunch time for grandchildren, Mỹ Tho 1942

The other side of this tatami lunch place was the dining room with a round table with chairs for ten people.

Born in the 1930's, my generation was the one that lived under numerous foreign occupations over the history of Vietnam. In the first half of my life, about 44 years after birth, I experienced a long succession of either foreign rule or involvement to include French oppressive colonial rule, Japanese imperial militaristic invasion, French bloody reoccupation of the colony, then later the costly American intervention which was first conditioned by the "Domino Theory." It was President Eisenhower who originally coined the term "Domino Theory" in response to a journalist's question about Indochina in a news conference on April 7, 1954. He explained that if the first domino (Vietnam) were to be knocked over, then the rest of the dominos (Laos, Cambodia, Thailand, Malaysia, the Philippines, Indonesia, Burma) would topple in turn.

As a teenager living in a colony, I did not know or understand the real history of the French presence in Vietnam. The general information and school books were purposely adapted to serve colonial rule and brainwashed the Vietnamese natives. I was taught in history classes to recite the phrase "nos ancêtres les Gaulois avaient des cheveux blonds!" (Our ancestors the Gauls had blond hair!) In what kind of country did I grow up during my teenage years?

Now, working on my memoir in the information age in America, I feel like walking into a gold mine of facts and information. Thanks to IT, Intelligence Technology's Google, I found so many interesting news items about my motherland's history from so many independent sources at the tip of my fingers. In the old days, I would have to go to the library and look for the same information. It has been fascinating for me to search for facts about the past of my country. The following is, in a nutshell, the complex history of contemporary Vietnam. For the first time, I can now say I am able to discover and understand clearly how the French came and occupied Vietnam.

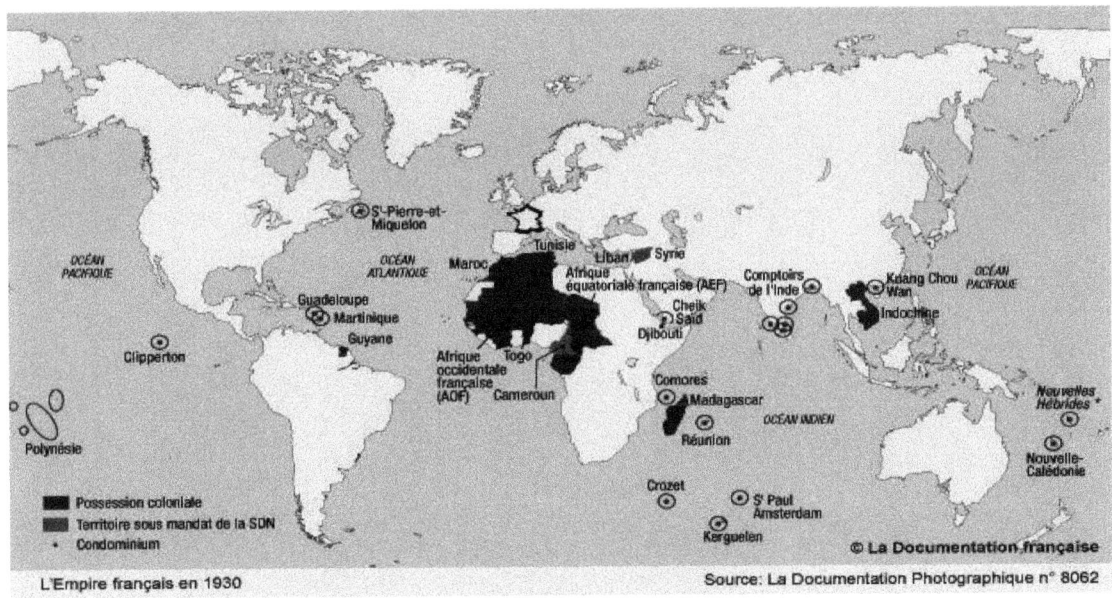

French Empire in 1930

French interest in Vietnam began in 1658 through the work of the Missions Étrangères de Paris (M.E.P) or Society of Foreign Missions of Paris, now known as Séminaires des Missions Étrangères. This institution was established by Rome's Sacred Congregation for the Propagation of the Faith in 1659 under the instigation of

Alexandre de Rhodes, a Jesuit priest. It was not a religious order but a grouping of secular priests and laypersons who were dedicated to missionary works in foreign lands. The priests sent to Vietnam went with the clear objective of proselytizing the natives to the Christian faith. Once in the country, they tried their best to adapt to local customs and establish an indigenous clergy while keeping close contact with the Vatican. In the 19th century, the Vietnamese Court's persecution of the missionary priests of the Society of Foreign Missions of Paris gave the French government a pretext to justify their military intervention in Vietnam. The admirals Jean-Baptiste Cécille and Rigault de Genouilly led an expeditionary naval force to Vietnam and captured Saigon on February 18, 1859, initiating the French conquest of Cochinchina (South Vietnam). More than a century later, on June 19, 1988, Pope John-Paul II canonized 117 martyrs of Vietnam including priests of the M.E.P, 11 Dominican fathers, 37 Vietnamese priests, and 59 of the Vietnamese laity.

For a number of complex reasons, the French government led by Napoleon III decided to solicit the help of Spain to conquer the six southern provinces of Viet Nam: **Biên Hòa, Gia Định, Định Tường (my birthplace) Châu Đốc, Hà Tiên, and Vĩnh Long** (my ancestral home town.)

Emperor Bảo Đại   *Empress Nam Phương*
(Reign: 8 January 1926 – 25 August 1945)

Establishment of French Indochina, 1887 - 1954

France gained control over northern Vietnam following its victory over China in the Sino-French war (1884–1885). French Indochina was formed in October 1887 from Annam (Central Vietnam), Tonkin (North Vietnam) and Cochinchina (South Vietnam) which together now represent modern Vietnam. The French were also able to include under their colonial rule the Kingdom of Cambodia and the kingdom of Laos. This latest kingdom of Laos was added to Vietnam and Cambodia after the Franco-Siamese War to form the so called (French) Indochina. The French formally left the local rulers sitting on their thrones to be called the emperors of Vietnam, kings of Cambodia and kings of Laos. In fact, all powers were in the colonists' hands and the local rulers acted only as figureheads.

My youth and my education were under a typical French Empire system. As a result, I knew French history and geography better than the average French citizen and not much about my own country. I knew very little about the 4,909 Km Mekong River running from the Tibetan Plateau through China's Yunnan province, Burma, Laos, Thailand, Cambodia and Vietnam. However, I could draw by heart and in detail the 1,000 Km Loire River and remember most of its Chateaux. Of course, the funniest and most unforgettable souvenir of my childhood has remained that juicy sentence recited by heart in my history class *("Nos ancêtres les Gaulois avaient des cheveux blonds!")* "Our ancestors, the Gauls had blond hair!"

French Foreign Legion and Senegalese soldiers; annual July 14th, Bastille Day parade in Saigon

To show off French military might and to impress the natives, France organized every year a spectacular show of force. I was always looking forward to the annual

July 14th, Bastille Day parade with the latest armament and the famous French Foreign Legionnaires. Their precision and cadence march was very spectacular. I saw also for the first time the scarred faces of the black Senegalese soldiers in the French colonial army. The prestigious 75mm canons always wrapped up the show off parade with tanks and amphibious vehicles.

Confused history of Vietnam during and after WWII

In a nutshell: The Germans occupied France. France continued to occupy Vietnam with Marshall Pétain collaborating with Hitler. By working with the Vichy French administrators, Japan used Vietnam as its war supply line. The end of WWII and the departure of the Japanese troops marked the end of French colonial rule but also the gathering of the dark clouds for the First Indochina War to begin!

My school life was in great turmoil due to the many political changes that modified my education program accordingly. From a French education system using Latin alphabets, I had to switch to the new Imperial Japanese program in **Kanji**, adopted Chinese characters. Then after the defeat of Japan in WWII, I went back to the previous French colonial system. My second language was Vietnamese then Japanese and back to Vietnamese.

This period was probably the most confused and complex one in contemporary history of Vietnam. The Japanese bombed the French in Vietnam. Then the Americans bombed the Japanese in Vietnam. The British captured the Japanese at the end. I witnessed under constant fear a clear cut case of a small country becoming a real pawn in a chess game played by France, the US, UK and Japan.

Roosevelt insisted on Vietnamese independence

President Roosevelt wanted to change the history of Vietnam by restoring independence to all the colonies in the world. During WWII, he announced his firm opposition to a restoration of the European empires in Asia. Franklin D. Roosevelt was more direct when he spoke about French Indochina. In January 1944 he wrote to Secretary of State Hull that "France has had the country… for nearly one hundred years, and the people are worse off than they were at the beginning… France has

 milked it for one hundred years. The people of Indochina are entitled to something better than that." An Allied victory would result in the dismemberment of the French Empire. (Franklin Roosevelt Conversation with Charles Taussig on French Rule in Indochina, March 15, 1945, from *Major Problems in American Foreign Policy, Volume II: Since 1914*, 4th edition, edited by Thomas G. Paterson and Dennis Merrill (Lexington, MA: D.C. Heath and Company, 1995, p. 190.) The American President wrote he was concerned about the brown people in the East. He said that there are 1,100,000,000 brown people. In many Eastern countries, they are ruled by a handful of whites and they resent it. Our goal must be to help them achieve independence. Roosevelt restated this foreign policy goal several times at various international conferences. However, in public, Roosevelt had to keep friendly relations between allies, notably with the British and the French as well. De Gaulle was well aware of the tensions in U.S. policy but had no means of gaining the sort of commitment from Washington that Churchill was receiving for keeping India. De Gaulle turned to his fellow imperialist for aid. The result was one of the most serious disputes in the Grand Alliance but eventually Britain's control of Indochina was turned over to France after the surrender of Japan.

During World War II, French Indochina was administered by Nazi Vichy France under Marshal Pétain. In South Vietnam labeled Cochinchina, I lived under French Rule while France itself was occupied by the Germans.

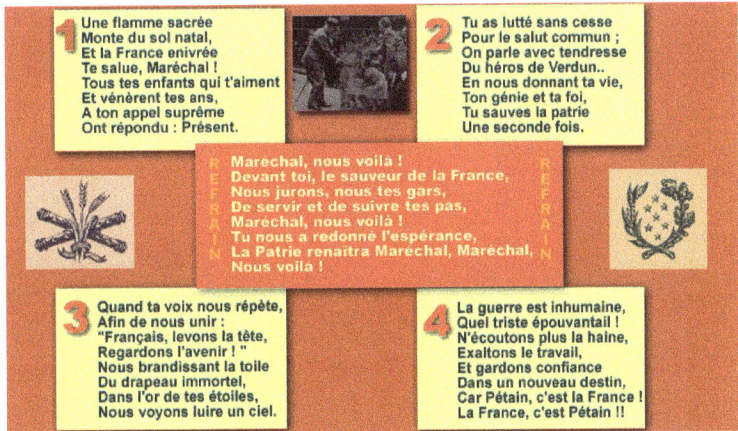

This song, 'Maréchal, nous voilà!' (Marshal, here we are!) replaced the French National Anthem, the 'Marseillaise'

From 1940 to 1944, every morning, I had to sing this new French patriotic song, while saluting the French flag in the center courtyard of the Mỹ Tho public primary school. I had to raise my right hand, Nazi style, to salute the French tricolor while singing this famous anthem at the top of my lungs. To this day, I still remember every word of it after 4 years of practice in the classroom during my early teens!

(English translation of the song)
Marshal, here we are!
Behind you,
The savior of France.
We swear this,
We, your boys,
To serve you and follow your footsteps.
The nation will be reborn
Marshal, here we are!

Now living "in the land of the free and the home of the brave" I feel very bad because I do not remember all the words of the Star-Spangled Banner. During WWII, the US wanted to cut the Japanese oil and raw materials supply line from Asia. As a result, Japan attempted to occupy Vietnam to construct military bases to strike against the Allies in Southeast Asia.

January 12, 1945, US Task Force 38 strikes Saigon

The United States did all it could to encourage Japan's fears. Viet Nam was now within easy reach of American fighter-bombers flying from Vice Admiral William F. "Bull" Halsey's Third Fleet, and later B-24s and B-25s taking off from Clark Field/Clark Air Base in the Philippines. On January 12, Halsey struck at Saigon as thousands of French and Vietnamese watched, hundreds from the city's roof tops. Five hundred American fighter-bombers sank four cargo ships and two oil tankers in Saigon harbor. Oil storage tanks along the river front exploded. Towering columns of black smoke reached a mile into the sky. In all, fourteen Japanese warships and thirty-three merchant ships were destroyed, the largest number sunk by the U.S. Navy in any one day in the entire war.

Japanese Empire 1942 in red

Japanese troops entering Saigon during WWII

On March 9, 1945, Japan ended nearly one hundred years of French rule in Indochina. Shortly before midnight on March 9 Japanese soldiers entered the governor general's palace and arrested French Admiral Decoux. Simultaneous attacks secured all the major administrative buildings, public utilities, and radio stations for the Japanese. French troops throughout the country were caught off guard. Whole regiments surrendered without a shot, though many others fought bravely even when encircled and out-numbered. Thousands of French were taken prisoners.

French sloop Admiral Charner sunk in Mỹ Tho 10 March 1945 by Japanese plane

I was thrilled to watch the Japanese planes diving and bombing this war ship in plain daylight in the Mekong River like in a movie.

Meanwhile, playing the role of liberators, the Japanese attempted to secure their hold in Viet Nam with the establishment of an "independent" government. On March 9, Emperor **Bảo Đại** was in Quảng Tân Province, entertaining French officials at a hunting party. Upon his return to **Huế**, he was informed by a Japanese commander that his country was free and asked to assume his full responsibilities as emperor. **Bảo Đại** convened his cabinet and on March 11 accepted the Japanese offer to head a new government.

It was a shock for me to see for the first time in my life, Japan controlling a French territory. In Mỹ Tho, I saw a half-naked French soldier tied to a post and exposed to the tropical sun by a Japanese MP. The Japanese administration played psychological warfare about the end of the white man dominating Asia.

My French schooling system was changed to Vietnamese. I had to learn to write Kanji, Japanese-Chinese characters for the first time. My second language was Japanese. Before the Japanese occupation, my first language was French and my second language was Vietnamese. This transition period was to be short-lived.

After two atomic bombs in Hiroshima and Nagasaki, Emperor Hirohito announced the surrender of Japan on August 15, 1945. On August 28, the occupation of Japan by the Supreme Commander of the Allied Powers began. The surrender ceremony was held on September 2 aboard the U.S. battleship Missouri, at which officials from the Japanese government signed the Japanese Instrument of Surrender, ending World War II.

On the same day, September 2, 1945 Hồ Chí Minh proclaimed Vietnam's sovereignty. Unfortunately, FDR died April 12, 1945. Roosevelt's insistence on Vietnamese independence faded away.

President Truman

De Gaulle

President Truman did not continue FDR's decolonization policy and was blackmailed by De Gaulle: "help me reoccupy Viet Nam and I will help you in NATO."

Hitler in Paris

French crying

French troops in Vietnam

Natives crying!

French reoccupying Vietnam with American aid: troop transports, tanks, amphibians and foods, GI's C-ration…

Already the French were regrouping, waiting to reenter the colony on the heels of the British occupation force's withdrawal from southern Vietnam. There would be a year of negotiations with Viet Nam, an attempt to establish a new relationship between Viet Nam and France. But the die was already cast. France, now under the political leadership of Charles de Gaulle, was simply unwilling to give away the 'jewel" of its empire.

After WWII, I remembered vividly the horrible day my father and I escaped from our home when the French Marines landed in my village of Rạch Miễu and burned our house with American flame throwers! We were almost killed that day by the French with US made machine guns. It was indirectly an act of war crime committed by the United States. If you were me, what would be your feeling toward the USA? It was a pity, a clear case of a small country being abused as a pawn by great powers.

As of April 1946, allied occupation of Indochina was officially terminated, and the U.S. acknowledged to France that all of Indochina had reverted to French control. Thereafter, the problems of U.S. policy toward Vietnam were dealt with in the context of the U.S. relationship with France.

The First Indochina War (also known as the French Indochina War)

French troops in 1946 in Vietnam

Map of French Indochina during WWII

President Harry S. Truman stepped up America's involvement in the French re-colonization of Indochina under the Truman Doctrine. A Telegram from **Hồ Chí Minh** to U.S. President Harry S. Truman requesting support for independence (Hanoi, Feb. 28, 1946) was never answered.

> The telegram from Hồ Chí Minh to President Truman stated, in part:
>
> *"I THEREFORE MOST EARNESTLY APPEAL TO YOU PERSONALLY AND TO THE AMERICAN PEOPLE TO INTERFERE URGENTLY IN SUPPORT OF OUR INDEPENDENCE AND HELP MAKING THE NEGOTIATIONS MORE IN KEEPING WITH THE PRINCIPLES OF THE ATLANTIC AND SAN FRANCISCO CHARTERS."*

Earlier, on February 16th 1945, Hồ Chí Minh had written a letter to President Truman asking for American assistance in gaining Vietnamese freedom. The letter closed with the remarks:

"We ask what has been graciously granted to the Philippines. Like the Philippines our goal is full independence and full cooperation with the UNITED STATES. We will do our best to make this independence and cooperation profitable to the whole world.

I am dear Mr. PRESIDENT,

Respectfully Yours,

Hồ Chí Minh"

[The letter was not declassified until 1972]

*Hồ Chí Minh, and Võ Nguyên Giáp (in white suit)
meet with Americans from Office of Strategic Services*

Bảo Đại's choice for prime minister was **Ngô Đình Diệm**, but the Japanese vetoed that appointment. A new Government of middle class intellectuals was formed. They quickly realized that Japan's defeat was imminent and that they, in the process, would be discredited. This chilling reality paralyzed the government, and it accomplished almost nothing of substance. Japan exercised real control over the country. After the final capitulation of the Japanese Empire in August 1945, Japanese troops still occupied Vietnam. But in what was perhaps a final attempt in defeat to keep "Asia for Asians" they surrendered to Hồ Chí Minh, rather than to Allied forces.

The French were gone, the Japanese had surrendered but meanwhile in Vietnam, a country deemed "incapable of self- government," order prevailed, not anarchy. There was no secret to the Hồ Chí Minh's success. He had simply done what generations of Vietnamese had wanted to do: proclaim **Vietnam's** independence.

The author of the Vietnamese Proclamation of Independence was none other than Hồ Chí Minh. As early as May 1945 Hồ had sought out a young American Lieutenant who had parachuted into the northern Vietnamese mountains with the OSS. "He kept asking me if I could remember the language of our declaration," the lieutenant later recalled. "I was a normal American, I couldn't." Eventually he realized that Hồ knew more about the American Proclamation of Independence than he did himself. On September 2, 1945, Hồ Chí Minh addressed a crowd assembled in Hanoi, and indeed, the entire world, with these words:

"We hold truths that all men are created equal, that they are endowed by their Creator with certain unalienable Rights, among these are life, Liberty and the pursuit of Happiness.:

"This immortal statement is extracted from the Declaration of Independence of the United States of America in 1776. "Understood in the broader sense, this means: All have the right to live to be happy and free. These are undeniable truths.

"We, the members of the Provisional Government representing the entire people of Viet Nam, declare that we shall from now on have no connections with imperialist France; we consider null and void all the treaties France has signed concerning Viet Nam, and we hereby cancel all the privileges that the French arrogated to themselves on our territory."

After eighty years of Western rule, Viet Nam was again independent and again united. That unity, more than just political, expressed the deepest wishes of the Vietnamese people. Hồ Chí Minh had taken control of the country virtually without opposition; a Việt Minh army of only two thousand men had been sufficient to secure the city of Hanoi for the new government. Within days, Emperor **Bảo Đại** abdicated, promising to support the new government as a private citizen. This peace in Vietnam was to be short-lived.

The CEFEO, Corps Expéditionnaire Français en Extrême-Orient was created in 1945 to rescue the overwhelmed "Indochina French Forces" fighting the Japanese. General Leclerc was nominated commander of the CEFEO in June 1945 and by August 15 received command of the Far East French Forces.

The CEFEO was made up of troops from the WWII free French Army and from the French Union colonial territories and the French Foreign Legion. The entire staff was from the metropole as well as from volunteers of the colonial airborne units. Already the French were waiting to reenter the country on the heels of the British occupation force in southern Vietnam. It was the beginning of the bloodiest and most destructive thirty years in Vietnam's history.

The Consultative Committee of Cochinchina consisted of four French notables and eight Vietnamese counterparts. On March 26th, 1946, the Committee appointed doctor Thinh to the post of interim Prime minister and entrusted him with the task of forming the Provisional Government of Cochinchina. The provisional cabinet made an official appearance before the public in front of the Saigon Basilica on June 2, 1946 with the following members:

- **Prime minister and Minister of Interior: Doctor Nguyễn Văn Thinh**
- **Vice Prime minister and Minister of Indigenous Armed Forces: Colonel Nguyễn Văn Xuân**
- **Minister of Justice: Trần Văn Tỷ**
- **Minister of Public Works: Lương Văn Mỹ (my wife's grandfather)**
- **Minister of Health: Doctor Khương Hữu Long (my uncle FOUR)**
- **Minister of Finance: Nguyễn Thành Lập**
- **Minister of Industry and Agriculture: Ung Bảo Toàn**
- **Minister of Education: Nguyễn Thành Giung**
- **Minister of Security: Nguyễn Văn Tâm**
- **Vice minister of Security for Sài Gòn - Chợ Lớn: Nguyễn Tấn Cường.**

Advisor: Hồ Biểu Chánh

Meanwhile the royalists continued to negotiate with the French on the issue of Vietnam's independence. In the Hạ Long Bay Agreement signed by Emperor Bảo Đại and the French High Commissioner Bollaert on December 6th, France recognized Vietnam's independence with a number of restrictions on foreign relations, defense and the status of the montagnards/ethnic minorities. In order to facilitate the transfer of total independence and the removal/renegotiations of the above mentioned restrictions, on March 26, 1948, Emperor Bảo Đại declared in Hong Kong the formation of the Provisional Central Government of Vietnam. At that time, five prominent personalities were considered for the prime minister post: **Ngô Đình Diệm, Lê Văn Hoạch, Khương Hữu Long(my uncle Four),Trần Văn Hữu, and Nguyễn Văn Xuân**. However, **Ngô Đình Diệm, Khương Hữu Long** (my uncle Four), and **Lê Văn Hoạch** declined because they did not agree with certain stipulations in the Hạ Long Bay Agreement. **Doctor Khương Hữu Long** recommended to Emperor Bảo Đại and the French Governor General the nomination of Mr. **Trần Văn Hữu.** Eventually, **Mr. Trần Văn Hữu** deferred to **Mr. Nguyễn Văn Xuân** who then became the President of the Provisional Central Government of Vietnam.

I was surprised to learn about the above history of Vietnam only in 2015, thanks to the Internet and Google. My uncle Four never mentioned to our family the fact that he was among the five personalities considered for the prime minister post by Emperor Bảo Đại.

On June 30, 1950, the first U.S. supplies for Vietnam were delivered. In September, Truman sent the Military Assistance Advisory Group (MAAG) to Saigon to assist the French.

French Union troops in 1953

USS Belleau Wood transferred to France in 1953 *French Union troops*

To reoccupy Vietnam, De Gaulle, after the German occupation, had not even ships to transport his troops overseas. In an irony of history, the French Indochina war was financed by the US: from ships to planes, guns, ammunitions, even C-rations. I knew well because I bought from the French soldier's chocolate and sliced bacon from their USA cans!

French 2nd Armored Division
French-marked USAF C-119 flown by CIA pilots over Điện Biên Phủ in 1954

A vicious war of independence erupted between the Viet Minh and the French until after the battle of Điện Biên Phủ in 1954. Two US pilots were killed in action during that siege. These facts were declassified and made public more than 50 years after the events, in 2005 during the Légion d'honneur award ceremony by the French ambassador in Washington.

After eight years of fighting and $2.5 billion [1954 dollars] in U.S. aid, the French lost the crucial battle of Điện Biên Phủ and with it, their Asian empire. That was the end of French Indochina Federation.

After the war, the Geneva Conference on July 21, 1954, made a provisional division of Vietnam at the 17th parallel, with control of the north given to the Việt Minh as the Democratic Republic of Vietnam under Hồ Chí Minh, and the south becoming the State of Vietnam under Emperor Bảo Đại, in order to prevent Hồ Chí Minh from gaining control of the entire country. A year later, Bảo Đại would be deposed by his prime minister, Ngô Đình Diệm, creating the Republic of Vietnam. Diệm's refusal to enter into negotiations with North Vietnam about holding nationwide elections in 1956, as had been stipulated by the Geneva Conference, would eventually lead to war breaking out again in South Vietnam in 1959.

My early years went through a very turbulent political period in French Indochina. It began with the Great Depression of 1929-39. Then I lived under constant fear during WWII when Hitler invaded France. French Marshall Pétain cooperated with the Germans and continued to occupy Vietnam. From 1952 to 1958, I was a student in the United States.

Ngô Đình Diệm, accompanied by U.S. Secretary of State, John Foster Dulles, arrives at Washington National Airport in 1957. Diệm is shown shaking the hand of U.S. President Dwight D. Eisenhower.

In retrospect, it was an eye opening for me to learn that truly the US went to Vietnam for its own interest more than for the democratization of Vietnam. It wanted to contain Communist China. I understand now why for a guerilla war, the US built the huge Cam Ranh Bay base with an airfield ready for B-52's and Boeing 747's in the early 60's.

Eventually, the Vietnamese domino did fall but the rest of Asia did not fall. South Vietnam paid a very high price for the American Domino experiment. I also wish my readers to remember the fact that F. D. Roosevelt wanted Europeans to decolonize their empires in Asia after WWII. *"He said that there are 1,100,000,000 brown people. In many Eastern countries, they are ruled by a handful of whites and they resent it. Our goal must be to help them achieve independence."*

As stated earlier, unfortunately for both the U.S. and Vietnam, right after FDR's death, Truman decided to finance several billion dollars for the French re-colonization of Indochina under his new doctrine. The end result was another 58,209 dead and 153,303 wounded of U.S. servicemen and women together with billions and billions of US dollars in American taxpayers' money for the so-called Vietnam war during three decades. That's a long story which will fill exactly the first half of my 86-Year Odyssey "East meets West" from the Mekong Delta to the San Francisco Bay. Let me now return to the 1930s and 1940s of my teenage years.

CHAPTER 2

Peaceful Life along the Mekong Delta

Calm and Romantic, a small village of the Mekong River

The Placid Mekong Delta

A man is, in part, the sum of his life experiences, and having lived though the most tumultuous time in the history of Vietnam, those events have been key in molding me into the person I am today. It is worth pointing out, however, that I was equally impacted by the tranquil and happy days of my youth growing up along the

Mekong Delta. In this chapter, I would like to set the stage of my early childhood and explain what life was like at that time.

What a Peaceful Life in the Mekong Delta

To fully understand the nature of the Vietnamese people, and the lifestyle of those living in the Mekong Delta, it is worth taking a look back at the migration of their ancestors into this area. In the 7th century, the small kingdom of Champa was formed along the coastline of central Vietnam where its people spoke the Malayo-Polynesian language. Starting in the 9th century, Cambodia, with its world renowned Khmer civilization, dominated Southeast Asia. Eventually, by the early 1800's, both Champa and what was formerly the southern part of Cambodia along the Mekong Delta, were conquered by the Vietnamese from the Red River Delta in the North. The migration of people moving from north to south in Vietnam can be compared to the westward movement of settlers in the United States.

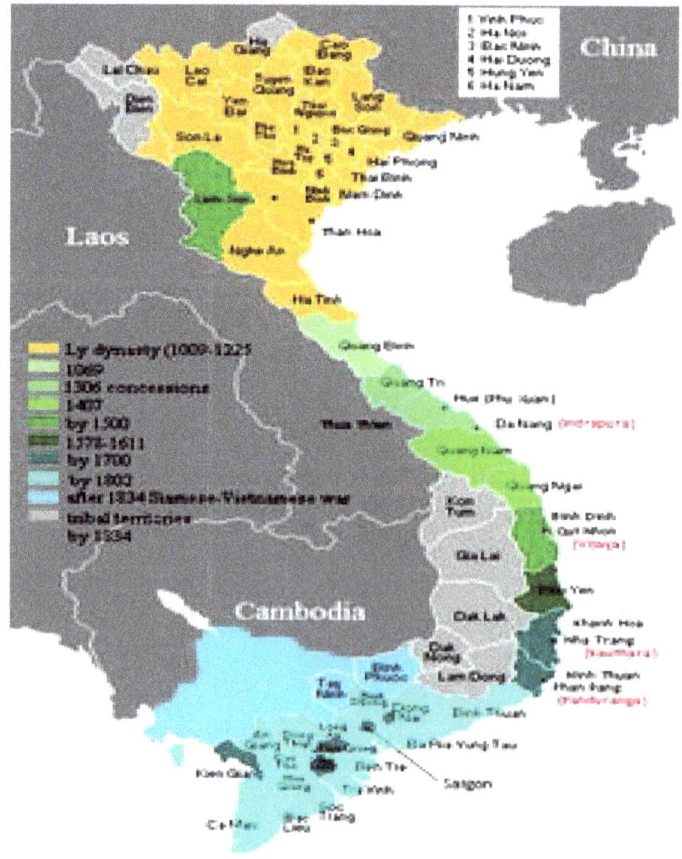

Map showing the conquest of Vietnam from North to South

The phrase "Go west, young man" came to symbolize the migration of people in the United States moving westward in the hope of staking out a plot of fertile farmland, where they could build themselves a new life away from the hardships and poverty from which they came. Similarly, in Vietnam, one of the principal motivations for the "March to the South" was the frequent and uncontrollable flooding of the Red River in North Vietnam. Political rivalry and unrest between various factions in the region also drove people to seek a better life in the south. Remarkably, the proud people of Vietnam were able to maintain their identity and national characteristics over the period of a thousand years of foreign domination spanning four Chinese dynasties. Eventually, the Vietnamese were able to overcome the Chinese invasion and the Vietnamese rulers rewarded their fighting men with farmlands in the south. Behind these aggressive pioneers came other settlers, meeting the resistance of the native Chams who gradually yielded their ground. The long "March to the South" could not be stopped. It continued from the 11th century to the mid-18th century. After nearly 700 years, Vietnam's territory gradually increased by three times from its original heartland in the Red River Delta to become the size and shape it is today. The Mekong Delta, with its Khmer Krom inhabitants of Cambodian descent, formally became part of South Vietnam as an outright French colony with the name Cochinchine by the mid 19th century. This history of the Mekong Delta explains the interracial blending of Chams, Melanesians, Khmers and Tiều Châu Chinese that make up the population of modern day Vietnam.

The gradual migration of people towards the south led to the blending of cultures, races and philosophies. This also brought about a transformation in the outlook and character of the people in the south. Overall, one can describe the South Vietnamese as more liberal, easy-going and open-minded than their brethren in the North. When you think about it, the people moving south were forced to be more accepting of new ideas and customs in order to get along with the rest of the population. On the flip side, the people in the north, having been dominated by the Chinese for a thousand years, had to secretly cling to their beliefs. They became accustomed to hiding their thoughts and feelings as a way to survive, and henceforth became more reserved and introverted by nature.

As in most hybrid cultures, the ideas and strengths of each population in the new frontier land were incorporated to everyone's benefit. For example the Tiều Châu Chinese, well known for their agricultural skills, used their knowledge to produce a bountiful food supply from the rich, fertile delta, thus enabling the people in South Vietnam to enjoy a richer life, different from that of their countrymen in North and Central Vietnam. And hence, the abundant Mekong Delta became a rich agricultural area with a peaceful and slow-paced lifestyle. This is the area where all of my happy childhood memories were formed.

Life was simple then. It was peaceful in the city, and even more so in the countryside. One could drive or take the train from the capital city of Saigon to Mỹ Tho, the gateway to the Mekong Delta, and then travel by boat on the countless little rivers to visit the tropical fruit gardens, see the peasants' houses on islets, and admire all the vast paddy fields. Like most people living in the Mekong Delta, I was raised on the water. The house where I grew up was actually in the peaceful village of Rạch-Miễu that was separated from the big city of Mỹ Tho by the mile wide Mekong River. My father built a 12x20 meter home near a ferry boat landing. Like many homes in the area, our house was half on land and half over the water, supported by concrete piers. The roof was made of water palm leaves, similar to thatch roof, which kept the house cool year round.

Back then, no one was stressed. No one was in a hurry. With the slow moving sampans on the rivers there was no rush hour. The people were not exposed to or tempted by consumer goods and their basic needs for food, clothing and shelter were provided by the fertile soil and the year round mild climate of the delta. In stark contrast to the big U.S. cities that I would later find myself in, there was no pollution from noise, dust, and car exhaust in the Mekong Delta.

To cross the many waterways slim "monkey bridges" were built at a minimum cost with the abundant bamboo available in any village. The name "monkey bridge" probably came from the assumption that people must be agile like monkeys in order to cross without difficulty. Some did not even have handrails.

Village scenes with cute "monkey bridges"

Peaceful Life along the Mekong Delta

"Monkey bridges"

Despite being a predominantly rural region, the Mekong Delta was one of the most densely populated areas in Vietnam with most of the land under cultivation. In addition to rice, the delta also produced an abundance of coconut, sugar cane, tropical fruits, flowers and fish.

Peaceful Life along the Mekong Delta

Working in the rice paddies

Kids taking care of their families' water buffaloes

Duck farm for egg production

Various Junks

Sampans and Water Taxis

Various Junks

Floating markets were common, and truly form an integral part of the daily life and culture of the Mekong Delta. The markets were busy, bustling and crowded like a floating city offering a broad variety of goods. Amongst the floating vendors, were small boats selling drinks and other products so that tourists and shoppers alike could enjoy a bowl of steaming hot noodle soup or a sweet-smelling cup of morning coffee while they shopped from their boats.

Our family would frequent the large Cái Bè floating market, near Mỹ Tho, which served as the hub for transporting local products to many regions in Vietnam. Hospitable local sellers at the market offered surprisingly cheap prices for fresh and delicious products. At the Cái Bè, and other floating markets in the delta, sellers did not cry out to invite guests to buy their goods. Instead, they attracted shoppers with strings of hanging samples hung above their junks. The larger floating markets operated 24 hours a day. At sunset, the market sparkled with lights from the junks and other boats with business activities carrying on until dawn.

Vietnam imported abundant live fish from the immense Tonle Sap Lake in Cambodia. The live fish were transported downstream using huge wooden barges with screened sides and big floats at either end. All the barges stopped at the port of Mỹ Tho where the fish would be loaded onto delivery trucks to transport them to Saigon early each morning.

Floating Markets

Floating Markets

Passenger boat for longer distance trips

Floating Freighters

Different sampan and boat designs

Water taxis

Peaceful Life along the Mekong Delta

Ferry boat

Local traffic

Typical delta town with an embarcadero

Map of the Mekong Delta with province names

Farmer's house

Harvesting lotus flowers and seeds

During my childhood, the fertile Mekong Delta was famous for its tropical fruits and flowers, and it remains so today. In the province of Bến Tre, coconut plantations and orchards were so dense that sunlight could hardly reach the ground. As a result, the girls growing up in this area were known for their delicate fair skin. In those days, Vietnamese girls did everything possible to avoid a suntan, and many covered their bodies completely from head to toe.

With water everywhere, houseboats were common, and rural peasants had a relatively easy life. They used the abundant water palms that lined the canals for making shelters. Rice was plentiful and cheap, and the numerous waterways provided an endless supply of fish and shrimp. They could plant vegetables and fruit trees near their houses, and each family could raise chickens and one or two pigs. Simple shirts and shorts sufficed for clothing in the mild year round weather.

Visitors to the region could take a cruise on the roof of a boat at sunset, looking at the distant and endless lines of coconut trees, with oil lamps flickering here and there, while listening to the cacophony of night birds, crickets, toads, and barking dogs. I have many happy memories of doing that with my family.

Palm-lined Canal

Low Cost Shelter from palm

Family Compound

Fishing

Mekong Delta houseboat

Tropical fruits on their way to market

Mangoustan

Cashew nuts (inside the black seeds at the end of the cashew fruits)

Jack fruits

Dragon fruits

Tamarind *Banana with its purple blossom* *Papaya*

Durian

Milky breast fruits

Star fruits

Trái cóc or "frog fruits"

Lecuma fruit

Custard apple. "Mãng Cầu fruit"

Chamoya

Pineapple

"Chùm ruột" fruit

Lychee fruit

Chamoya

Hairy fruits

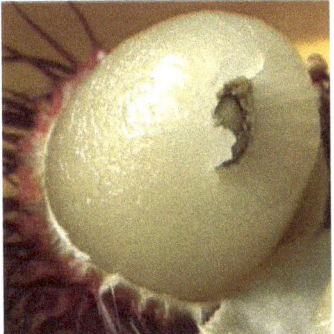

Sapotilla

Tropical plums

Tropical plums

Village fruit cart

Small quantities of fruit were sold in the local village markets, but most fruit produced in the Mekong Delta was consumed in other parts of Vietnam. The fruit was brought to the wholesalers' warehouses by boat, and then it would travel by truck to the capital city of Saigon, or by rail to Mỹ Tho.

Rice field

The Delta, made up of low lying alluvial deposits near the end of the 4,500 km long Mekong River, was the rice bowl of Vietnam – producing three harvests per year. During my youth, the rice was harvested by hand and sun dried. Manually operated wooden equipment with circular fans to produce air flow was commonly used to blow sand, dirt and straw away from the rice. Prior to World War II, Vietnam was the world's greatest exporter of rice.

Harvesting the rice

Rice processing equipment

Drying paddy

During the 30's and 40's, China was poor and underdeveloped, and they had no means to build dams on the upper reaches of the Mekong River. Therefore, the alluviums from the high mountains of Tibet, and the thousands of miles upstream of Vietnam provided natural organic fertilizers for the whole region. Later, however, communist China built so many dams upstream of Indochina that the water flow in the Mekong was radically reduced, creating panic downstream because salt water began to flow back into the Mekong Delta. As a result, fish, fruit and rice production all suffered.

The Delta was not a primary battle ground during the Vietnam War. However, after the communists took over the South and imposed their rule over the entire country they created great hardships including acute food shortages. This was not mitigated until 1985 when the Hanoi administration introduced its "renovation" policy. The people in the Mekong Delta area were then able to cultivate their fertile land to become the great rice bowl of Vietnam once again. Vietnam is now the world's second largest exporter of rice.

Life in the cities during my youth was also unhurried and calm. In Mỹ Tho, much of the architecture was French by design. The most impressive building was the residence built for the chief of the province.

Residence of French Province Chief

It faced our local "Champs Elysées" where the military parade was held each year on the 14 of July, Bastille Day. Other structures built by the French included the beautiful Catholic Church, the court house, an administrative building, the barrack, the maternity hospital and the stadium, plus a tall reservoir to supply the city with a gravity fed water distribution system. There was also an impressive club house built over the Mekong River where French officials would go to enjoy happy hours.

During colonial times, the omnipresent French police exercised strict local gun laws and other tight controls over the native population. I have vivid memories of the French chief of police inspecting the town by bicycle in his impressive khaki uniform with his big revolver in a shiny leather case at his belt.

From a practical viewpoint, however, it can be said that people throughout the country were able to live safely, day and night. My father, for example, a well-known businessman in town, could apply only for a simple compressed air gun for bird hunting. As a result of this tight security, there were almost no guns in the entire province. Nor were there any hoodlums or street gangs. One of our family's businesses, a jewelry store, operated for 50 years without any security problems, or even a security guard.

Each week my father took a train to Saigon, carrying an ingot of gold in his leather briefcase that weighed several kilos. He would take the ingot to the Indochina Bank where it was tested for gold content and exchanged for cash. The gold came from used jewelry sold to our family store by people from all over the province. For years my father traveled alone and never worried about his safety. It was very a different time.

My father would give me a bit of pocket money for helping him melt all the used jewelry. We would use a furnace heated by mesquite charcoal, and my job was to crank a hand driven high speed fan that would keep the fire hot enough to melt the gold. The liquid gold that would end up in the crucible was then poured into a rectangular steel mold. The end product was an ingot that looked like a gold brick. This is the gold that he would bring to Saigon each week. I remember that he took the early train. I was allowed to walk with my father to the station. We would stop at a nearby restaurant for breakfast where I would have my favorite – café au lait (coffee with milk) and a delicious "Hủ Tiếu Mỹ Tho," Mỹ Tho Noodle Soup, a specialty famous in the whole of Cochinchina even in today's Vietnamese communities in America. After breakfast, I returned home for my schooling. I would then walk back to the station to meet my father at 6 pm.

Every so often, as a special treat, we would return after dinner for a very special train ride. You see, when the train stopped at Mỹ Tho station, it had no room to turn around for the return trip to Saigon. Therefore, the train had to back-up to an area in the outskirts of the town where it could make a 180 degree turn. Then it would back up once again into the station to get ready for the early trip to Saigon the next morning. That short trip to the country side was always an exciting ride for me!

Mỹ Tho-Saigon train 1938

I can go on and on with the numerous and very pleasant recollections of my teenage years in the Mekong Delta. I often say to myself that I am quite fortunate being a Vietnamese from the Mekong Delta instead of from North or Central Viet Nam. It is well known that, compared to people from Hà Nội or Huế, the "Saigonese" are more open-minded and tolerant. On the other hand, they are rather loudmouthed and at the ready for a brawl but also quick to forgive and forget. That could be an honest description of myself, a youngster from the Mekong Delta and a typical Saigonese!

Little did I know during my teenage years in the 1930s and 1940s that the waters of that great Mekong River were running through my hometown of Mỹ Tho and then across the vast Pacific Ocean to reach the shores of San Francisco Bay, my future hometown in America, my adopted land during the 1970s.

Quite a journey, I must say, but this had to wait for "Điểu" - the little Mekong Eagle - to begin and complete its flight across the Pacific Ocean, my 80-year Odyssey that I have been trying hard to remember and describe in the following chapters of this book. The year 2015 marked exactly the 40th anniversary of my arrival at Camp Pendleton as a refugee and the beginning of the second half of my life as an American citizen. I still sadly miss the Mekong Delta with the precious memories of my beloved parents, relatives and childhood friends there in the land of my ancestors.

CHAPTER 3

My Childhood Fun in the Mekong Delta

Air View of Mekong Delta with 9 estuaries

The Mekong Delta also known as the Western Region, viewed from the air, is a very flat country with lowland rice fields and brown alluvium water. It includes Cần Thơ capital of the West and 12 provinces: Long An, Tiền Giang, Bến tre, Vĩnh Long, Trà Vinh, Hậu Giang, Đồng Tháp, An Giang, Kiên Giang, Sóc Trăng, Bạc Liêu and Cà Mau.

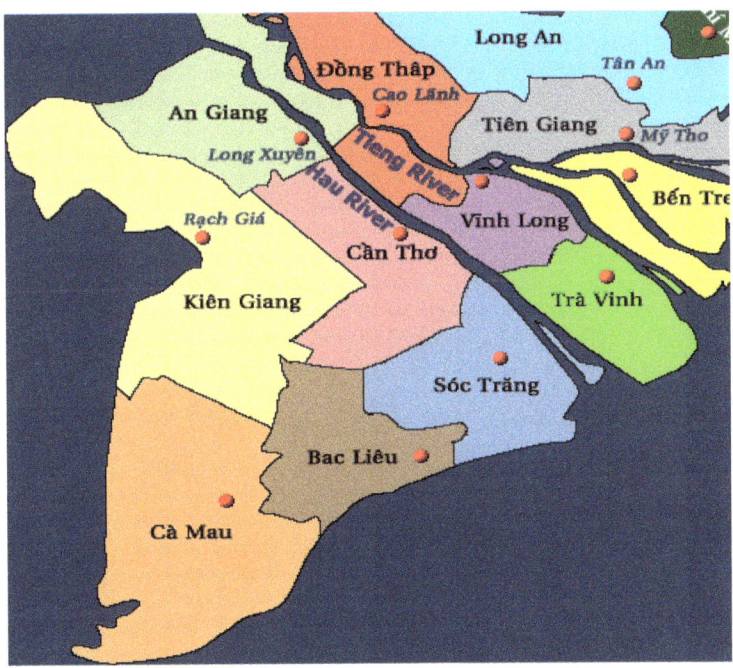

Map of the Mekong delta with province names

Village road in the delta full of exotic, tropical plants

My recollections of the Mekong Delta are still quite vivid in my mind. I remember well the kind of life and the inhabitants there, most of them having a hard existence as farmers, artisans and fishermen. Life clustered along the banks of the rivers or canals with simple dwellings of various structures built from whatever materials they could find. Consequently, the architecture in the Mekong Delta offered a large variety of landscape from place to place.

Typical houses in the delta

Typical houses having water palm leaves for roofing and mooring sampans at the side to serve as a means of transport and "wooden garages" for storage as well. Life on the banks of the rivers meant some houses built half on land and half above the river to keep cool year round and also to have the God given "running water" for bathing and other household uses!

House built half on land and half above the river

Villages along the Mekong River with rice fields and fish ponds

Typical river traffic in the delta

I have a great many memories as souvenirs of my childhood fun with my father in the Mekong delta. I feel lucky to have had as father, an outdoor person who really loved nature. Most of the weekends, he took me to the countryside with its attractive rice fields, colorful tropical orchards and animated canals and waterways. The photos show those beautiful places with their interesting activities.

Rice Mill visit

One of our family businesses was a rice milling factory in the suburb of Mỹ Tho city. My early engineering curiosity started by observing how the complex equipment transformed paddy to brown rice. Then a polishing machine converted brown rice into white rice. The by-product was bran used to feed pigs. I remember my father asking my Sister Four to prepare pudding with bran and chocolate for dessert. I realize now that it took the West many years to begin marketing bran as a high quality nutrition product in the supermarkets. I also learned that another by product of rice milling was husk to be used as fuel for cooking and for industrial kilns. It was also most helpful to the farmers as fertilizers for their vegetables gardens.

Village mini rice mill

Brick Factory visit

My father showed me various factories to guide me to my future, especially to my career in engineering later on. I loved to go out with him to visit the clay brick factory near our rice mill.

Brick factory

Junk full of rice husk

Rice husk is used as fuel for local factories such as brick kilns or copra coconut dryers

Worker carrying rice husk to brick factory as fuel

The visit to a brick kiln was more fun because I could take home a lot of good clay to make my own toys like cars, motorbikes, miniatures homes, cooking utensils, houses for fighting crickets … I learned how peasants used clay and a wooden mold to make bricks by hand at a fast rate. After drying those clay bricks in the sun, they baked them in the red brick conical kilns shown in the photos above. The fuel used was either wood or rice husk from nearby rice mills.

My father's program of showing me how people worked in the village continued with the processing of coconut copra and the production of "Nước mắm," "the national sauce" made of fresh fish/salt and used for cooking. By the way, "Nước mắm," is the Vietnamese counterpart of soy sauce of China, Japan and Korea, the so called "Chopstick group." Please note that among two hundred countries of the world, only four eat with chopsticks.

Fish Sauce Factory visit

Fish sauce is an amber-colored liquid extracted from the fermentation of fish with sea salt. Fish is fermented by alternating a layer of fish and a layer of salt in cylindrical wooden containers shown below. The best quality of fish sauce in Vietnam comes from Phú Quốc Island and Phan Thiết because those two regions have excellent anchovies as an ingredient. In the Mekong Delta only soft water fish "Cá linh" and "Cá cơm" are available for producing fish sauce and the quality is not as high as anchovies. For "Nước mắm" containers, originally people used baked clay containers (See photo below) but nowadays, glass or plastic bottles have become more popular.

"Nước mắm" or fish sauce factory with cylindrical wooden containers and small clay pots

Rice Paper (bánh tráng) Factory visit

Rice paper is made from steamed rice batter which is then sun dried. Vietnamese rice paper for wrapping food is comparable to flatbread tortillas used for thousands of years in north, northwest and northeast Mexico where they are a staple, as well by many southwestern US Native American tribes.

Rice grinding: Soaked raw rice is ground with water into slurry by this very simple machine. Farmers use a cylindrical hand operated stone grinder to make flour the main ingredient of rice paper. (Photo of stone grinder and making "bánh tráng")

Stone mill

Making rice paper

Making thin "bánh tráng" rice sheets: the "bánh tráng" maker sits on a low stool to spread the batter onto a cloth that's stretched over a wide pot of boiling water. After the batter has been thinly spread, a lid is used to cover the rice sheet. The resulting sheet is steamed for probably about 30 to 45 seconds. The round sheets are taken outside and spread out on bamboo platforms to dry in the sun. Once they are ready, the sheets look like a piece of opaque paper.

Drying the rice paper: As stated, to dry the cooked rice sheets, the racks are brought outside and placed under the hot sun for a day. The woven pattern of the racks gives the rice papers their distinctive appearance, which factory-made ones mimic. The dried, finished rice papers are stacked up, then tied into smaller stacks and taken to market.

Rice paper being dry in the sun on bamboo platforms

This rice paper is used extensively in Vietnamese cuisine for wrapping the famous "Chả Giò" or "Imperial Rolls" and "Gỏi Cuốn" or "Salad Rolls (See photos)

The "Gỏi Cuốn" (Salad Rolls)   *"Chả Giò" (Imperial Rolls)*

Coconut Copra Factory visit

Copra is the dried meat, or kernel of the coconut used to extract coconut oil. It also yields coconut cake which is mainly used as feed for livestock. Almost everywhere in the delta you could see coconut trees either in plantations or grown with other fruit trees around the house. Normally farmers transport their coconuts to the processing factory by junks because it is the most efficient and inexpensive way. (See photo below)

Coconut copra factory

The Mekong Delta is the land of the coconut. Coconuts EVERYWHERE and the people of the delta depend on the coconut for EVERYTHING. It's used for fuel, candy, liquor, roofing, bags/purses, carved into cheesy looking souvenirs, brooms, brushes, treating insect bites… you name it and they will turn the coconut into a use for it.

Coconut supply to factory by junks

Worker separates fiber from nut

Workers use a simple metal tool to separate the fiber from the hard spherical nut. When the nut is split in half, the juice is collected for making caramel used in cooking. The white meat is solidly attached to the hard shell. Copra is produced by removing the white meat from the shell, breaking it up and drying it. Different methods like smoke drying, sun drying or kiln drying are used to dry the copra. Sun drying requires little more than racks and sufficient sunlight. Halved nuts are drained of juice, and left with the meat facing the sky. When the white meat is heated in a dryer or kiln, it shrinks, loosens itself from the hard shell and becomes dark meat.

White meat inside the coconut shell

Dry brown copra

When the nut is split in half, the juice is collected for making gourmet caramel by boiling and concentrating it in a big wok. The hard shell is used in industry to produce activated carbon. Under French colonial rule, Vietnam was known for its export of copra to Marseilles for the production of the famous soap at 72% coconut oil.

Artisan Sugar Factory visit

Sugar cane being harvested in the Delta

Sugar Cane Trucks, neatly stacked for trip to sugar mill

A load of sugar cane on a canal trip to a sugar mill

In the village an artisan sugar mill juice extractor is either hand operated or on a bigger scale, driven by oxen, water buffalo or a small engine. Juice is boiled to evaporate into very thick syrup and then poured into molds. After cooling it becomes a solid sugar cake to be cut into tablets.

Small sugar mill

My Other Kinds of Kid's Fun in the Mekong Delta

All of the previous fun came from my father's ideas of educating me through his guided tours of life activities in the villages. By observing how people worked for a living, I was exposed to the meaning of the positive purpose in life. What form of contributions would I choose for my future?

My rubber sling shot gun

It was a very interesting toy because it allowed me to go bird hunting with kids of my age. We looked for doves, wild pigeons and a lot of other tropical wild birds whose names I didn't know. With this rubber propelled toy I used to shoot down sweet tamarind and mangoes along the tree-lined streets of my home town. Not all the trees had sweet fruits and that was another challenge for my search. For bullets, I took wet clay from the brick factory, made spherical balls and baked them in the kitchen charcoal fire.

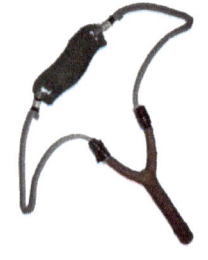

Rubber sling gun

Cricket

Catching crickets in the rice fields, feeding them and matching them up for a good fight was another interesting pastime. The kids from the neighborhood got together with their collection of crickets and organized exciting matches. The critical point was how to choose equal and fair opponents for the matches.

Pairing for equal size

Glass jar was our fighting ring

Fighting crickets in a glass jar

Crickets fight

I did not forget to mate my warriors with female crickets as I believed it helped the male fighters relax before the fight. After my daily routine of feeding them, I spent a lot of my time observing and selecting the best ones by looking at their color, listening to their chirping and watching their movements. In a fighting container, handlers stimulated their cricket's whiskers using a straw stick to make the insects annoyed and aggressive until they revealed their tough teeth shaped like hooks. When both crickets were in the mood for a fight, a small panel separating the insects was lifted and their fierce fight began. The fighting lasted just a few seconds and winner and losers were determined by the cricket that started to run away from the battle or stopped chirping. When a fight began and the crickets rubbed their wings singing their fighting song to challenge their opponent, I felt like I myself was going into the boxing ring.

Fish Fighting

Fighting fish were bred to bring out their violent characters

Cock fighting

Children's fun in the village
Matching equal pair of mini size fighting cock

My Childhood Fun in the Mekong Delta

I have lived in the U. S. almost half a century and I understand that in the West, cock fighting is illegal and considered cruel. However, this deep rooted Vietnamese custom may make me look like a monster child if in my memoir I consider cock fighting as a kid's fun. "Other land, other custom" and I recall Rudyard Kipling's famous quote: "Oh, East is East and West is West, and never the twain shall meet." In the west, children have many sophisticated toys. As a kid in a French colony in Southeast Asia in the 30's, my toys were primitive. They came from nature like fighting crickets, fighting fish, fighting cocks. Other toys were made of clay. By the way, crickets, fish and cocks do fight among themselves and by themselves voluntarily in nature. I just want to mention here the kinds of fun that I was able to enjoy during my childhood in the Mekong Delta and was not at all affected by the accusation of cruelty against animals. In all fairness, I must say that I am much horrified by what I can see everyday on TV in the US showing terrible bloody fights between human beings in boxing and wrestling!

Living in the Mekong Delta, I was able to discover that cockfighting was common there as it was throughout all of Vietnam. Kids loved to have their own cocks and enjoyed taking care of them. In the early stage, the younger roosters would battle for a victory with their blunt natural spurs or lack thereof. Real fights start only after the cocks have reached maturity and they attack each other using their full grown natural spurs which could have become quite pointed by then. (See photos of fighting cocks)

 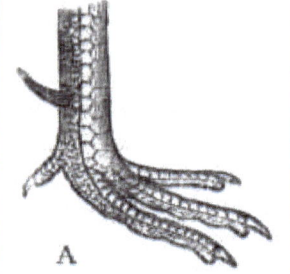 

Spur of fighting cocks

The spurs could be a very deadly weapon. I loved to raise the fighting cocks from the egg stage to chicks and kept the ones with the best colored feathers. Before the fight I sharpened the spur with a very sharp knife.

One more exciting kid fun was to go bird hunting with my father. During the rice harvest season, we hunted doves that were feeding in the paddy fields. But the most prized bird for hunting was the eagle. It was most challenging because an eagle always stayed on the top of the tallest tree of the area. Under colonial time my father was authorized to own only air guns with one type of tiny lead bullets. It was very difficult to hit an eagle with such short-range air guns. With the eagle's long feathers on the wings, my grandfather used to make beautiful hand fans. For lunch in the country side, there was also the excellent village "Bánh Canh Cá Lóc" or "Snake Head Fish Noodle Soup". This was a top choice fish in the delta on account of its delicate flesh. Many times, after lunch, my father cut a few large banana leaves and let me have my siesta on those green sheets.

Very Special Kid's Fun

I had my unforgettable, unique souvenir while visiting my cousin's rice field in Vĩnh Long, an important town in the Mekong Delta. He owned 50 hectares of well maintained rice fields. Typically, there was a dike around the perimeter of the property to control the level of water during the rice planting season. Wild fish and crustacean could come in from the Mekong River with the high tide but could not get out of the rice field because there was a one way butterfly valve locking them inside. They grew up naturally in the rice field for the whole year. A network of small canals crisscrossed the property. There was the once a year rural festival called "Chắc Đập" or "Empty the Dike" day when all his farm hands got together to celebrate.

50 hectares of rice fields crisscrossed by irrigation canals

Only one deeper canal left to retain all the fish of the vast rice field

As you can visualize from the two photos above, when all the water from the crisscrossing canals was drained, fish and crustacean were caught in the only muddy canal left. The water of this canal finally flew out via a screened gate. Our fun was how to get rid of the mud on the top of the fish and lobsters left behind! The solution was rather simple. We made a three foot diameter cylindrical roll of rice straw the width of the canal. Five of us kids stood behind the straw roll and pushed it forward to displace the mud.

Cá Lóc "Snake head fish"

Cá rô "Gourami"

Mekong fresh water lobsters

Right under the layer of mud you could see nothing but lobsters and fish. Now what to do with this delicious harvest? The quickest and best way was to line up the lobsters and fish on the ground, cover them all with rice straw to grill them and wait for the blue lobsters to turn into the red color and dinner was served! What a most delicious meal of my childhood in the village of the Mekong Delta in the middle of the rice field.

Due to lack of refrigeration, all the farm hands worked went full speed to process the total harvest using salt as preservatives and huge baked clay jars to contain all the fish.

The exceptionally plentiful and beautiful life in the Mekong Delta had to share eventually the sad fate of the entire Vietnamese nation in war. It can be said that life in the Mekong Delta and in Vietnam from north to south was relatively peaceful under French colonial rule including even the short period of the pro-German Vichy government of Marshal Pétain. World War II did not touch Vietnam much until the arrival of the Japanese troops. Compared to the former French colonial administrators, the Japanese occupiers were more violent and cruel although having the yellow skin like the Vietnamese! The end of World War II in 1945 was the beginning of the most tragic pages in the history of the Vietnamese people who had to endure widespread death and devastation with the return of the French expeditionary forces. This so-called First Indochinese War ended after the French defeat at Điện Biên Phủ in 1954 and the partition of Vietnam at the 17th Parallel by the Geneva Accords into a communist North Vietnam and a non-communist South Vietnam. In the following five years, there was relative peace in South Vietnam but by December 1959 the communist leaders in Hanoi decided to "liberate" South Vietnam by both political and military means. That was the beginning of another long war involving the gradual intensification of US military intervention in the defense of South Vietnam against this armed aggression by

North Vietnam. The Vietnam War, which ended on April 30, 1975 with the fall of Saigon to the invading North Vietnamese troops, was the first of its kind as a combination of conventional warfare and guerrilla warfare to include systematic acts of terrorism on a large scale.

Throughout the Vietnam War from 1960 to 1975, the Mekong Delta area was not subject to the great battles up to divisional levels between the regular units of the NVA (North Vietnamese Army) and the ARVN (Armed Forces of the Republic of Vietnam). Still, the communist rule which was imposed on the entire country immediately after their takeover in 1975, created great hardship throughout, including an acute shortage of foodstuffs. This was not mitigated until 1985, when the Hanoi administration had to introduce its so called "renovation" (đổi mới) policy.

The people in the Mekong Delta area were then able to cultivate their fertile land to become again the great rice bowl of Vietnam which has helped Vietnam to be nowadays the world's second largest rice exporter. That rich and beautiful Mekong Delta was the one I used to know and have cherished from the time of my childhood. If you look at it from a bird's view high above, the Mekong Delta is like an enormous flat pancake laced with countless small waterways and, of course, with the wide and long Mekong River originating from the mountains of Tibet and throwing itself finally into the vast Pacific Ocean in South Vietnam to reach its American shores in California where I am now. Very much like my long journey of over eight decades from my hometown of Mỹ Tho in the Mekong Delta to San Francisco Bay!

PART II

Learning the French Way

CHAPTER 4

A Taste of Competition at Le Myre de Vilers, Mỹ Tho

Main Entrance of «Collège Le Myre de Vilers» Mỹ Tho 1944

I have many members of my family living in France as French citizens. I want to avoid any misunderstanding. My writing about the French colonial system mistreating native Vietnamese reflects only the true nature of historical facts. I happen to have lived under that 20th century of exploitation of Asia by Europeans. The majority of the French people do not always share the policies of the French government, especially in the French colonies. Under the French Empire, two rules were clear: Divide to conquer and the least educated the natives, the easier to govern them. My junior high school was named after the Governor of Cochinchina, Le Myre de Vilers. French Indochina was divided into Cochinchina, Annam, Tonkin, Laos and Cambodia. For the whole Cochinchina, the south of present day Vietnam, the education system included only two junior high schools or "colleges" in French, located in Cần Thơ and Mỹ Tho provinces in the Mekong Delta and four senior high schools or "Lycées" in French namely Pétrus Ký, Gia Long, Chasseloup Laubat and Marie Curie in Saigon, the capital of Cochinchina. There was no university. In the old days, "Cochinchinois and Annamites" were required to go to Hanoi, 1,072 mi (1,726 km) up north to attend Hanoi University, the only institution of higher learning in Indochina. It had purposely no engineering school, in order to keep manufacturing as a monopoly for exporting French manufactured goods to its colony.

School's 130th anniversary 3/17/1879--3/17/2009

School's 130th anniversary 3/17/1879--3/17/2009

Candidates came also from the surrounding provinces of Bến Tre, Tân An, Gò Công, Vĩnh Long, Sa Đéc and Long Xuyên.

Just to study in a junior high, I had to first pass a formal exam for the Certificate of primary school level, "CEPCI" "Certificat D'Études Primaires Complémentaires Indochinoises."

To pass this formal exam, I had to register to compete for a place in Mỹ Tho's junior high. It was a very tough screening process at a very early age because there were too many candidates for very few available seats in the school.

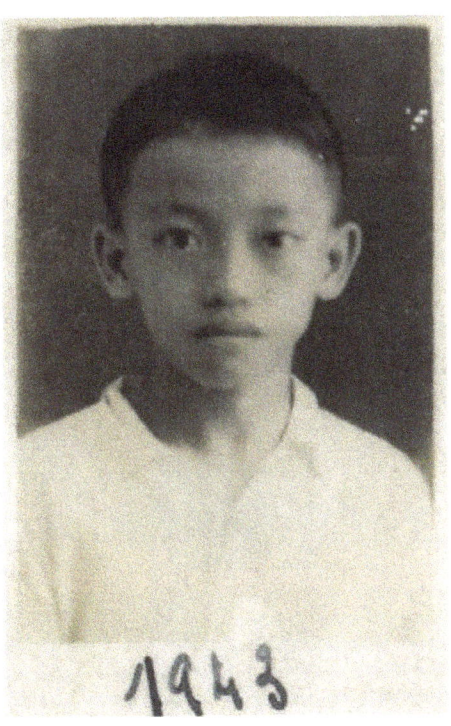

ID photo required for primary school exam, 1943

I was very nervous and afraid of failure because there was no where else to continue my education, unless I moved to the capital city of Saigon to attend some private institutions. At 13, living away from home for schooling was not appealing at all. Fortunately, I passed that severe selection process. That was my first taste of tough academic competition and it was the initial launch of my non-stop, long journey full of challenges to the very end of my student life in the United States. This rough journey started in Mỹ Tho junior high, continued on to Dalat at the prestigious French Lycée Yersin, then to Lafayette College in Pennsylvania and ended at MIT, Cambridge, Massachusetts.

Students in black and white school uniforms in front of the main gate, 1944

Students in freshly painted building

A campus corner with old building

Statue of Scholar Nguyễn Đình Chiểu

Girl students' uniform "Áo Dài"

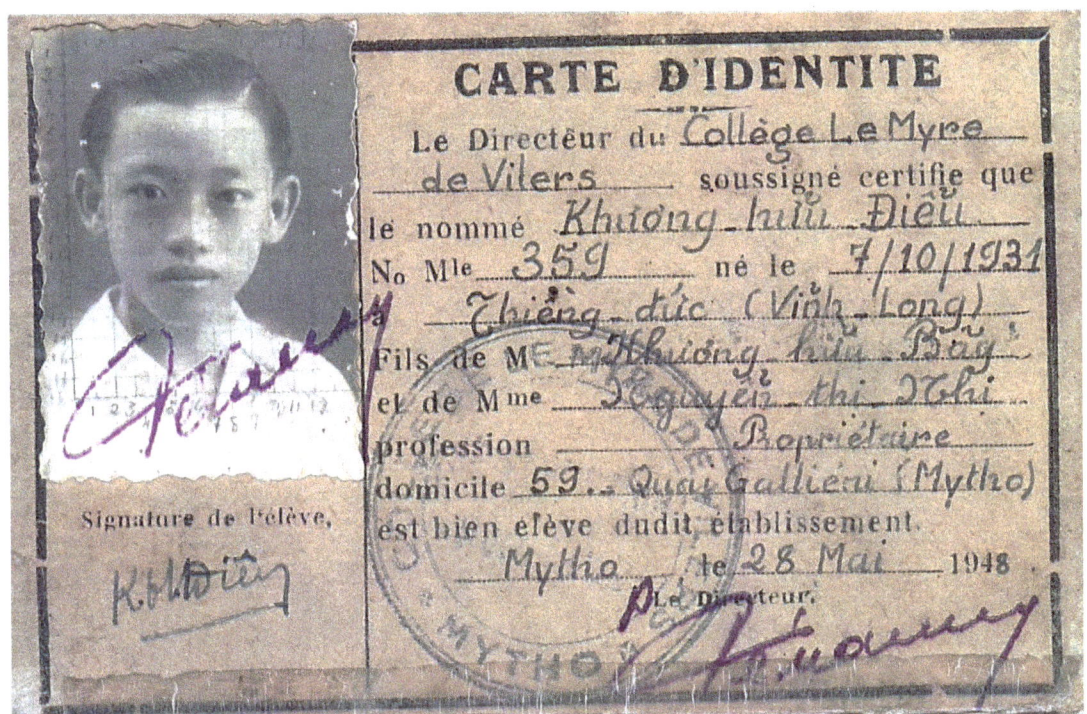

My ID card in Junior High School, in French (1944 -1948)

Old classroom building & courtyard

Studying in primary school was fun with its free style voluntary system except for the final year exam for the Certificate. A failure meant the end of schooling because there was no other institution in town. Now, in junior high, student life was completely different. I was subject to a lot of new disciplines, namely:

1. School uniforms, *Vietnamese style,* collarless white pajama shirts, white colonial cork hats and wooden sabot.

2. Clothing uniform, but in *Western style,* composed of white short sleeve shirt and shorts with white socks, white "Bata" (French brand name) tennis shoes and white helmet called "casque colonial."

White colonial cork hat, 1944

3. Every weekday, two homework sessions one in the early morning and one in the evening on the campus under the watchful eyes of a "surveillant d'etudes" or "study supervisor."

The school discipline was under very strict control of a "Surveillant Général" or "Principal Supervisor" who happened to be an Indian French citizen.

Each morning, the students were required to salute the French tricolor flag before classes started. For special occasion, the uniform shirts had two black insignias at the collar, with the embroidered gold letters CMV - for Collège Le Myre de Vilers. On week-ends the intern students in their nice, prestigious white uniform made a promenade tour of the town under the watchful eyes of supervisors. "Interns" were students who lived in the campus dormitories. As a student living off campus, I had to wear the school uniform like the interns for special school events.

1947

This was my junior high school western uniform; missing were the hat, a "white casque colonial" and white tennis shoes with white socks.

As an extern student, I lived with my parents in town. However, every day I had to wear the school uniform and at 7AM started my one hour and half of homework in school together with the intern students. In the evening, after dinner I had to come back for another one and a half hours of homework. No conversation or distractions were allowed during those homework sessions. Discipline was very strict compared to what I see now in the US schools.

Fast food restaurants did not exist. Near the school entrance, a few squat food vendors gathered around the light of the town lamp post to sell breakfast to extern students. For breakfast, I typically had the following choices: hominy grits or sticky rice served with white coconut chips, brown sugar and roasted sesame seeds, or fish soup with rice noodles. There were no paper napkins or plastic
wares. Food was served on skillfully wrapped green banana leaves. A more western breakfast of French baguette, pâté and headcheese with pickled carrot and daikon (white radish) came from a merchant in his tricycle shop. He had his own acetylene lamp for lighting.

Baguette   *Pâté foie*   *Head cheese*

Classrooms with green courtyard and tall trees to maintain a comfortable temperature under the hot tropical sun

All the courses were taught in French by "professors" as we all called them. They were either graduates of Hanoi University or French universities. One professor was responsible for math and sciences, one for geography and history, one for Vietnamese literature, one for drawing and one for physical education. All were Vietnamese except one French professor from Paris teaching French and French literature.

For each class, a student with nice and neat hand writing was chosen to keep the accounting book for grades of all students. I remember my friend Phạm Thế Hùng was assigned to that prestigious task. Hùng happened to be the tallest student in my class. We became friends for the next four years and beyond. In fact, he married my first cousin while I was a student in the US. He came from Chợ Gạo district about 30 km from Mỹ Tho. He lived in a boarding house just outside the campus. I used to study with him because at home, the jewelry store was not quiet with a dozen goldsmiths working. At the end of each month, there was an official ranking of the students for each class. That put a lot of pressure on me because I was very afraid to be at the bottom of my class! My parents tacitly did not expect that. It was my very first taste of stressful academic competition. Everybody tried to be on the "top of the basketful of crabs!" Now I find this expression amusing since in real life the chef may cook the top crab first!

I wanted to be number one in my class, and so I began to learn the art of competition at this early age. The reality was rather simple but hard to accomplish. In a nut shell, most students tended to study only the subjects they liked, so I figured out that if I studied both what I liked and didn't like, then I would get a higher total monthly average. It was fair, simple and straight forward. To be number one, I did not have to be the smartest student in the class, but only needed to observe the law of the survival of the fittest. It usually required 10% inspiration and 90% perspiration, and I practiced this philosophy with perseverance. I believed that this simple formula kept me where I wanted to be during my long academic journey from Mỹ Tho junior high to Dalat Lycée Yersin, all the way to college and university in the United States. I had to be a steady hard worker and a well rounded one. Like in a lot of famous schools many students wanted to be on top.

My home in Mỹ Tho was known as "Tiệm Vàng Khương Hữu" or in English, "Khương Hữu Jewelry Store." A dozen goldsmiths worked there full time during the week and some also worked during the weekends on rush jobs. It was a noisy and very distracting place to do my school homework. They sang folks songs or played guitar during lunch and break times. I loved also to listen to their jokes and interesting stories. My escape was to go to some of my classmates' homes and study with them. They became my buddies and on weekends we got together either in my parents' orchard and rice mill or in the city park along the Mekong River.

At school, the rote system was used extensively. I specially liked the mental calculation class of the famous professor Phùng Văn Tài. It was a smart way to do quick mental calculation. However now that I know the U S system, I prefer it and believe it is more open to innovation than the strictly old-fashioned rote system. Students who learn through reasoning and understanding are able to transfer their knowledge to tasks requiring problem-solving with greater success than those who learn only by rote. Vietnamese and Chinese educators hold high the tradition of rote learning as being an integral part of their culture. In Singapore, with the introduction of the Integrated Program, the government is making attempts to move away from rote learning, at least for the more able students. In many fields such as mathematics and science it is still a matter of controversy as to whether rote memorization of facts such as the multiplication table or the boiling point of water is still necessary. Progressive reforms - such as outcome based education – which emphasize the elimination of rote learning in favor of deep understanding have produced controversy among those favoring traditional rote methods. In some American text books, such as the K-5 mathematics curriculum, the subjects of investigations in Number, Data, and Space of TERC [Technical Education Research Centers (TERC), Inc.] omit rote memorization in favor of conceptual learning.

I noted that Vietnamese students including myself rarely asked tough questions of the teachers. This might have been due to our upbringing in Confucianism with its great respect for the elderly - in particular the teachers. By tradition, teachers are the equals of parents. So, in the classroom there seemed to be just a one-way street in the flow of information. No heated debate with or challenging of the teachers.

I remember most my math and science professor. A graduate of the University of Paris, he was very confident in the teaching of his courses and kept the class alive with little jokes every so often. Probably he liked Vietnamese noodles so much that he always told the students to order for him "Một tô hũ tiếu, hai tô nước lèo" "One bowl of noodles with two bowls of broth." He told us a lot of short stories from his student days in Paris. He invariably walked to class from his home a mile away in his white suit, white shirt and white colonial cork casque. Another unforgettable teacher was professor Tài from North Vietnam. His very strong, funny accent in French was the talk of the class.

I had the most fun with a few close classmates. We enjoyed picking all the tree ripened tropical fruits in my parent's orchard. We swam in the muddy river and caught wild shrimps using a specially designed bamboo baskets along the water palm trees on both sides of the waterway. Most rice mills had a pigeon farm because those birds fed on the paddy that fell out of the paddy jute bags stored around the mill. On special occasions, we used a ladder to climb up the pigeon nests to catch young squabs. They were considered real delicacies in the Vietnamese menu.

Pigeon nests

We would also sit together along the Mekong River embarcadero and enjoy the sunset and the cool breeze.

The first three years of school were less stressful than the last one. During my fourth year, I was really obsessed with studying for the final exam in order to earn the diploma known as DEPSI (Diplôme d'Études Primaires Supérieures Indochinoises), which was very highly rated in the French Empire. In the French system, none of the grades you earned during the entire four years counted towards the DEPSI. Regardless of how well I did in my last four years, I had to pass the final exam to get the diploma. Thank God, I made it with a "Mention Bien," the highest rating of my promotion. I was valedictorian or "Major de Promotion" in French. De facto, I was nominated by my school to go to French Lycée in Saigon to participate in the Brevet Élémentaire exam, which had the same rating in France, unlike the Vietnamese DEPSI. I was shocked to discover that I had to know the fundamentals of music called solfège, a system of attributing a distinct syllable to each note in the musical scale.

I had to sing a French song and beat the time with my finger for this exam. Solfège is a form of solmization, commonly characterized in English-speaking countries by the syllables: do, re, mi, fa, sol, la, ti, do. I looked for the best music teacher in town and went through a crash course. It was an adventure for me to go to Saigon, the capital city, and take the exam at a French school. A really intimidating trip. Our family owned a bus company connecting Mỹ Tho to Saigon. I took the evening trip and slept on the roof of the bus. It parked in front of my Sister Six's home. At night, the Vietnamese use a special mat made of reed similar to a tatami to sleep in and avoid the mosquito bites. After I took my breakfast at my Sister's home, I headed straight to the French Lycée Marie Curie for the exam. I had no problem with all the regular courses but felt very scared of this music test. A French lady asked me to sing a song while beating the time followed by several questions on solfège. I felt all shook up but it turned out OK in the end. That was a liberating moment.

No one in my family celebrated my achievement in passing the exam, probably because they expected no less. However, my father's friend and neighbor, pharmacist Trần Văn Khanh, acknowledged my academic success and asked my father to go to Saigon's famous Albert Portail bookstore on Catinat Street to choose the best French desk set for me. What a great gift for my academic milestone!

By tradition, the school organized a very important year-end variety show performed by the students themselves. The program included a French theatrical play such as Cinderella or "Barbe Bleu," tap dancing, standup comedians, singers, chorals … ending with the traditional farewell song "Choral des Adieux," the French equivalent of *Auld Lang Syne*.

In retrospect, after four years at Mỹ Tho junior high school, I learned the fundamentals for academic success: study discipline, rigorous competition, and perseverance among students more intelligent than myself. I also learned that in addition to academic success, some social activities were necessary to maintain some equilibrium in life. Academic genius without social contact can lead to an unbalanced life. All work and no play makes Jack a dull boy.

As mentioned above, a big city like Mỹ Tho had no senior high school. That was typical of the colonial system restricting the number of educated natives for easy governing. However, even at the junior high level, it was Quality even in the absence of Quantity in education. I must admit that for the prestige of the French empire, the colonial government unfailingly maintained the high quality of its "diplôme" or diploma. The proof was that with my modest French schooling in Mỹ Tho, I was able to move on to another French school, the prestigious Lycée Yersin in Dalat, which would pave the way later on for me to perform successfully at MIT in America. My unbelievable academic journey actually began at this junior high Le Myre de Vilers in my hometown of Mỹ Tho.

CHAPTER 5

Da Lat & Lycée Yersin

When East and West first met

Sweat and Tears
The Maiden Flight of the Eagle:
10 percent inspiration and 90 percent perspiration

In Vietnam, people from the Mekong Delta looked at Dalat as the most beautiful town and an ideal place for vacations. When I was twelve years old, I was very happy to join my parents on a visit to Dalat as tourists. The long 400 km trip in a French 4-door Citroen was spectacular. Dalat was a mile high and known as the Pearl of the Highlands. We drove over two picturesque, winding passes at Blao and Prenn. Coming from the hot, flat delta, I was very impressed by high mountains with thick, evergreen tropical forests. Unique also were the vast, well kept green plantations of tea and coffee in the Blao and Djiring plateaus regions. It was also the first time in my life that I saw pine forests like in Europe with many farming areas producing what we called Western flowers, fruits and vegetables, such as strawberries, plums, leeks, potatoes, butter lettuce, chicory, endives, artichokes, gladiolas, mimosa, tulips…None of those existed in the tropical delta. Even the names of the lakes, streets, hotels, and auberges were like in France: Au Sans Souci, La Savoisienne, Lang-Bian Palace, Rue des Glaïeuls, Rue des Roses…lac des Soupirs, lac St Benoit, lac des Cygnes…It was like a mini France from my geography text book. In the street, people dressed up with woolen jackets, wool caps and gloves. Many wore suits and ties. Morning fog was thick as pea soup. I had never seen anything like that. Spring was very colorful with pink blossoms.

Pink Cherry Blossoms

When I finished my Junior High School in Mỹ Tho in 1948, I was forced to leave home to continue my education elsewhere because there was no high school in the entire Mekong Delta. Here was the same old story: the least educated the natives, the better the control for the French Empire. And I was one of those natives.

I was lucky to have the help of my Uncle Four, Dr. Khương Hữu Long. He had a farsighted view for the future of the children in the family. He completed all the paper work for my admission to Lycée Yersin, located in Dalat, 400Km from home. In the 40's that was a long distance in Cochinchina, former South Vietnam. Fortunately for me, my uncle Four owned a villa in Dalat and I was able to stay there to go to school with his two children: Khương Hữu Hội, now a retired pharmacist and Khương Hữu Thị Hiệp, wife of Dr. Hồ Trung Dung, former head of Saigon Từ Dũ Maternity hospital. Uncle Four was the first Minister of Health of Vietnam under President Nguyễn Văn Thinh, March 26, 1946 - November 10, 1946. He was my very first Good Samaritan because without his aid, I would have hit the low ceiling of my academic potential very early in life. By the way, he told me that President Thinh committed suicide while still in office on November 10, 1946 because "he was being compelled to play a farce," by the French.

Academically, Lycée Yersin was a show case, a prestige institution of the French secondary school system. All the teachers were French of high standards recruited directly from Paris. Two blacks, French citizens from the Martinique Islands, taught gymnastics. The only two Vietnamese teachers were in charge of Vietnamese literature and Drawing classes. Students had the choice of either English or Vietnamese as a second language.

Uncle Four, my Good Samaritan Dr. Khương Hữu Long

Main Campus Building

Many students were either French or French citizens with a group of Vietnamese and a few Laotians and Cambodians. Students spoke mostly French among themselves. The campus and its architecture were very modern and attractive (see photos). In fact, the main building on the campus was declared by the International Union of Architects (*Union Internationale des Architectes*, or UIA) as one of 1000 best world projects of the 20th century.

I grew up in Mỹ Tho on the left bank of the Mekong River. It was the second largest city after Cần Thơ, capital of the West. Mỹ Tho was well known for its famous Collège Le Myre de Vilers (named after the Ex-Governor of Cochinchina). The collège is the first level of secondary education in the French system. In 1948 when I graduated from there with the French "Brevet Élementaire" and the" DEPSI" (Diplome d'Études Primaires Supérieures Indochinoises), I had reached the highest level of education available in town. Though a highly rated junior high school, all the students and teachers were Vietnamese with the exception of Mme Poitiers teaching French. Students spoke only Vietnamese among themselves and were less fluent in French. Besides, they spoke French with a strong local accent.

I had to leave home for *high* school. I did not have much of a choice because of the restricted colonial education policy. Why? Simple answer: There were three Basic Colonial Rules.

Higher education promotes leadership which leads to "Liberty, Equality, Fraternity" the national motto of Métropole France. But this was against the colonial policy. Therefore:

Rule # 1: Less educated natives mean better and easier control. The least schooling in the colony, the better for the Colonial Administration. In my days in 1944-51, for all of French Indochina (Cochinchina, Annam, Tonkin, Laos and Cambodia) there were only 9 high schools; four in Saigon; two in Huế, capital of Annam; and three in Hanoi, capital of Tonkin (with one and only one limited university there). Even the future King of Cambodia Norodom Sihanouk had to go to Saigon for his *high* school at Lycée Chasseloup Laubat. There was no engineering school in the whole of Indochina. Why? Because manufacturing and industry were the monopoly of France for the export of its manufactured goods.

Rule #2: Divide to govern. Vietnam was divided into Tonkin, Annam and Cochinchina.

Rule #3: The French were first class. They created local second class citizens. In fact the Chinese in Vietnam were second class ahead of the Vietnamese.

In the 40's, the Vietnamese students in Lycée Yersin were more or less the "cream of the crop" from Tonkin, Annam and Cochinchina. Academic competition seemed fairly keen and healthy. Coming from a Vietnamese speaking school to a

French speaking campus, I was handicapped with my foreign accent but adapted myself quickly to the new system.

My long term objective was to study engineering abroad and my obsession was to do well in mathematics and the sciences for my future professional requirements. I got a head start in this field; instead of enjoying my summer vacations in 1948, I went to Saigon, staying at my sister Three's home. She and my brother-in-law Professor Nguyễn văn Khuê were managing their own Lyceum near Cầu Ông Lãnh, Saigon. I was taking additional math courses with the famous professor Vương Gia Cần. Each day, I rode my bike to my math teacher's house in Phú Lâm, 6 km away from downtown Saigon with my friend Bùi kiến Thành, son of well-known Dr. Bùi kiến Tín, famous for his "Eucalyptus oil," "Dầu Khuynh Diệp Bác sĩ Tín" in Vietnamese.

Life in Dalat required woolen clothing due to mile high cool weather. Later on, I discovered that my classmates from the North and Central Vietnam were much better dressed than those from the delta because they came from a cooler climate.

Life changed drastically for me from Mỹ Tho in the flat, tropical Mekong Delta to Dalat on the mile-high cool plateau. The greatest change was the town of Dalat itself. The French, in the 1930's, wanted to create Dalat as the most beautiful city in French Indochina, a show case of French civilization, a mini France in its Empire. In fact, if you look at the city planning, landscaping and especially the architecture of its buildings, you can see that France accomplished a beautiful job.

Why then Sweat and Tears in a New Beautiful Dream Town? Because I was too young to understand the psychological shock resulting from the complexity of my new life. According to the laws of nature, when you uproot a tree from a fertile soil in warm tropical climate and transplant it to a poorer soil in the colder climate of a mile-high plateau, the tree has a hard time to grow or even to survive. *I was that tree.* Overnight, I lost my wonderful, exciting, entertaining lifestyle among members of my family and friends. It was the first time in 17 years that I was transferred from my happy home in the Mekong Delta to a cold new environment. Dalat was completely different from Mỹ Tho. In the beginning, I did not know how to resolve my unexpected nostalgia problem and started to cry.

I suffered home sickness coupled with loneliness. There was no medicine for my nostalgia. It was too much for me to bear. I kept missing my own comfortable routine and always remembering the good times: lunch and dinner time, enjoying meals around the family round table with my parents, my brother, sisters and cousins. Every so often, we had pleasant, entertaining family guests. During the day time, I had the company of many schoolmates, childhood buddies and many friendly goldsmiths working in my parents' jewelry store. Their shop was attached to our home by a short walkway. I loved to join them, watch them working. Each goldsmith was an artist by himself. They were very different from workers of the assembly line. For instance, the goldsmith-sculptor transformed a piece of gold into either the classic design of Dragon, Lion, Turtle, Phoenix (Long, Lân, Qui, Phụng) or the Four Seasons theme of Cherry Blossom, Pine, Chrysanthemum and Bamboo. (Mai, Tùng, Cúc, Trúc). It was fascinating to watch a goldsmith transform a piece of solid gold into beautiful jewelry in a few hours. While working, they also sung popular folks tunes. I loved to watch them making bracelets, earrings, chains, and necklaces… all types of Vietnamese traditional jewelry. They were all my good friends. The most respected of them all was the one working with diamonds. Why? Because others could make a mistake with gold and could correct their mistakes. With diamonds, everything had to be right the first time. A little error might break the diamond and became a catastrophe. That was why the customer always sat next to the goldsmith while he installed his or her diamond. A very meticulous, tedious but perfect job.

Early every morning, they showed up to work well dressed with their fancy felt hats. Because of the tropical, hot weather, they changed to shorts and tee shirts, their uniform in the shop. Many even worked with their culottes, short trousers without shirt for comfort. Their conversation was very amusing to me---a lot of folksy stories. At lunch time, they played chess or guitar besides reading the newspaper. There was no television in those days. On week-ends they took me to the town stadium to watch exciting inter-provincial soccer games.

My parents also managed the bus company Khương-Hữu connecting my hometown to Saigon, the capital city 70 KM away. The bus drivers were also my friends. Every morning, local merchants shipped fresh vegetables from Mỹ Tho to the Saigon market. Around 6 AM, they loaded fruits and vegetables contained in bamboo baskets on the roof, yes on the roof of the bus. That was their routine way of doing things. The bus driver was having breakfast while his aid took care of the loading. I liked to have coffee with my friendly bus driver because he volunteered to teach me how to drive a bus. We could do that very early in the morning, say 5 AM. There were no cars in the streets. You can see how life was so exciting for a kid like me driving a bus! That was how I learned to drive and got my license at an early age.

My parents owned also the rice mill Khương-Hữu with a few acres of fruit tree plantation in a suburb of the city. On holidays and week-ends, I invited my schoolmates to spend our good time picking the delicious, tree ripened tropical fruits at the rice mill plantation. We swam in the river in front of the mill. It was really fun all day! Now, from this enjoyable, active social life, I really felt depressed to leave all that behind me so as to continue my education, 250 miles away from home.

The reason for me to dwell so much on the way of life I led in Mỹ Tho, my hometown, was to bring out the profound difference as well as the sudden clash between the Vietnamese customs and traditions and the way I was to behave and conduct myself at the Lycée Yersin. I had to conform with French *savoir faire* and Western culture. Little did I know then that a very serious process of genesis was about to begin in my heart and mind when "East Met West" so concretely for the first time.

In retrospect, my academic success or failure depended so much on how I could solve my homesickness-nostalgia problem and how able was I to adapt myself to the very French way of life in Dalat, particularly the new school called the Lycée Yersin.

Lycée Yersin and Lac des Cygnes downtown Dalat

Why choose Lycée Yersin in Dalat highlands as my high school, 400 KM away from home? Because it's one of the best and located in the most beautiful city of South Vietnam.

Main building of campus with typical morning fog

The landscaping and architecture of Dalat was in the style of the French Empire period.

Da Lat Church

Lac des Cygnes with club house La Grenouillère and villas

Morning fog

Da Lat Railway Station

The Da Lat Railway Station, built in 1938, was designed in the Art Deco style by famous French architects Moncet and Revero.

At the Railway Station with TTQuan, one of my schoolmates in 1951

School Life

My first impression of Lycée Yersin was unforgettable. Just to get there from my home by bicycle was a scenic trip. I went through a beautiful, refreshing pine forest, then a route along the calm Swan Lake with a modern hotel followed by a final steep climb to a hill dominated by an award winning tall red brick building (See photos).

Pine forest near home and Swan Lake

Lang-Bian Palace Hotel, near Swan Lake

Swan Lake Downtown

Lycée Yersin Campus on the hill

Lycée Yersin Campus on the hill above Swan Lake

The award winning building is at the center of the photo. My new bicycle itself was different from my old one. The many hills around town required bicycles with brake and shift levers combined. I later found out that this high school in Vietnam had a campus similar to a typical college campus in the New World with dormitory and stadium. The students at Yersin were classified as "Internes" with sleeping facilities in dormitories on campus and "Externes" living in town. I was in the same class with the following Vietnamese friends: Hoàng Cơ Lân, Tôn Thất Niệm, Vĩnh Mậu, Tạ Ngọc Châu, Yvonne Bửu, Simone Huệ…

A brief mention here about these classmates of mine some six decades ago at that French Lycée Yersin in Dalat: unlike me, they continued with the French academic system. I have learned that many of them have retired in France: HCLân, former Chief Surgeon of the Airborne Division, then Commandant of the Military Medical School of South Viet Nam. TNChâu, Education Specialist, UNESCO Paris, Robert Vĩnh Mậu Nuclear physicist, Professor Emeritus at Université Pierre et Marie Curie, Y.Bửu Mathematician, Professor Emeritus École Polytechnique Paris. TTNiệm, MD, former minister of Health, retired in California. I have no news from S. Huệ owner of a great Maternity Hospital, Phú Nhuận, Saigon.

At the Lycée Yersin it was natural that I was expecting some kind of discrimination or some condescending because I came from a strictly indigenous Vietnamese school and needed to integrate myself into a truly prestigious French school. What I discovered may shock some readers. Because my field of study was mostly in Math and Sciences, considered as a universal language, I was not much handicapped in the use of the French language in a French school. I was however quite surprised that the French students in my class were constantly behind me in grades. I was then talking to myself about being smarter than the children of a race that claimed to be superior and imposed colonial rule on the Vietnamese.

L to R: 1ˢᵗ row: Du, Châu, French student, Simone Huệ; 2ⁿᵈ row: Điểu, Lân, De Rougny: 3ʳᵈ row: Phú, Vĩnh Mậu, Thông. Standing: Mme Marty our Physics teacher

Lycée Yersin, 1950 Mme Marty Physics class

Mme Marty and TNChâu, Physics class 1948-51

Schoolmates on week-end cycling trips 1948-51

Du, Lân, Điểu
Schoolmates on week-end hiking trips 1948-51

Ankroet Dam 1948-51

Cao-Điền, Thận, Kiệt, Điểu

I learned some new social customs; even in high school, teenage interns were served wine with meals on week-ends, something unheard of and illegal on American campuses. I had a chance to learn this later during my overseas study. The ground floor of the main building had several ping pong tables. Rain or shine, the "externe" students liked to come early to play games before classes. Physical education and gymnastics were required subjects. We had two black monitors from French Martinique to run this department. My first year in this school was a little unusual because most students spoke French on the campus. For my 17 years of schooling, this was a first. At first, I did not feel comfortable because of my foreign accent. But with time, speaking French became second nature.

Besides, my objective was to be the best in Mathematics, Physics and Chemistry for my future career in engineering. For other courses, I did not mind to be among the crowd. The school had a tradition of printing every year a famous "RED BOOK," listing top ranking students in every course offered, with annual special awards from celebrities. The equivalent of Valedictorian title in the USA was "Prix d'Excellence" in the French system.

My first year was only a warm-up or tune-up year for a neophyte transferred from a Vietnamese to a French school. Besides I was handicapped by nostalgia! The next two years of my hard work seemed to pay off. I had learned and gone through a tough lesson. It was always 10% inspiration and 90% perspiration. Thank God, I had a very happy ending. I was awarded two consecutive years the "Prix d'Excellence" at Lycée Yersin in 1950 and 51.

In my final year, the greatest surprise was the Prize from SM Norodom Sihanouk, King of Cambodia, and then the Prize from the Mayor of Dalat followed by the Prize from the Association of Students' Parents of Chasseloup Laubat, Marie Curie and Lycée Yersin," names of the three French high schools in Cochinchina. My greatest academic milestone happened at the year end French Baccalaureate in Mathematics. I passed with the rare "Mention Bien," the first in six years at Lycée Yersin. Also one of the big surprise prizes was my Sports medal in gymnastics from France OSSU. (Organization Scolaire Sportive Universitaire.) For this, I gave thanks to the training by my father. Very early in life, almost everyday my father forced the children to get up at 6 AM and began our 20 minute walk to the Mekong River swimming pool. He chose that way to keep us healthy and we continued to maintain the healthy tradition of regular physical exercise for life.

I still feel extremely moved now each time I remember all such advice from my father. I will never forget that at the end of my last year at Lycée Yersin, my father made a special, tiring 400 Km trip from Mỹ Tho to Dalat to support my morale during the stressful final exam in 1951. He surely felt that I might get homesick, which combined with loneliness, would hurt my potential in the tough exam.

It was such a tremendous challenge at the time for a young Vietnamese seeking better education under the harsh colonial rule and competing fiercely with guys from very powerful and rich families. Little did I know then that my good performance and the high honors at the famous French school Lycée Yersin would later lead me to a then unbelievable and extraordinary destiny!

My father was very proud of my accomplishments but there was no celebration in the family. In his Vietnamese Confucian tradition, he did not manifest it explicitly like many fathers in the West. Maybe his nature was more introverted than mine.

Life in Da Lat 1948-51

Nostalgia

My uncle Four had a medical office in Vĩnh Long city, Mekong Delta, 460 Km from Dalat. Whenever he took a vacation near me in Dalat, I felt a chance to rediscover my familiar home life. Daily, after dinner he asked us to walk with him for more than an hour around the peaceful town and gave us some helpful advice for a successful life. We all shared delicious meals with him because, with his presence, the menu was upgraded a lot and the cook, chị Ba Vú, was known in our family as one of the best for Vietnamese and French specialties. However, most of the time, my uncle was busy working in Vĩnh Long and for those long periods of his absence, I fell back into my homesickness.

Fortunately, one day in a French literature class, God seemed to give me a break; I found an unexpected solution to my depression caused by nostalgia. We were studying the great romantic authors of the 19th century: Victor Hugo, Chateaubriand, Lamartine, Musset, Sand and Vigny. In particular, the Poetic Meditations by Lamartine grouping the famous poems celebrating nature in its affinities with the human sensibilities fascinated me greatly. My excellent French teacher did convince me with the poem "Le Vallon" from Lamartine that Nature is a reliable maternal refuge. It was the image of consolation, of protection of a mother. These images were so great because they had a constant, permanent character with the words *"always," "the same"*. I remembered by heart this part of the poem:

"Méditations poétiques"
(1820)

« Le Vallon » (extrait)
« The Small Valley » (extract)

Mais la Nature est là qui t'invite et qui t'aime ;
Plonge-toi dans son sein qu'elle t'ouvre toujours
Quand tout change pour toi, la nature est la même,
Et le même soleil se lève sur tes jours.

"But Nature is there that invites you and loves you;
Dive yourself into its breast that's always opened to you
When everything changes to you, Nature is the same,
And the same sun rises over your days.

This poem marked an opposition between the stability of nature versus the human instability. Whenever I felt depressed mostly because of nostalgia, I took my bike and visited Nature with all its beauty around Dalat known for its rolling hills, calm lakes, serene forests...The softness of those hills, green in spring, colorful otherwise, soothed parts of me, healed me in ways I never planned or anticipated. And the sun on those hills – the *sun*! It made me weep sometimes. It was the silent presence of those hills and that sun that I needed. They were a prayer and an answer, both.

Lamartine's poem had sparked my own consciousness of the way the earth was healing and has healed me. The sun and the seasons have spoken of hope or blessings to me already. Lamartine praised Nature close to God. Later I discovered that in California John Muir had similarly observed that Nature may heal and give strength to body and soul.

From that exceptional "Lamartine class," no one can take that nostalgia remedy medicine away from me. Better than that, the love of Nature continued to lead me to new horizons. I started to enjoy the Japanese way of appreciating Nature to the point of creating Nature in Miniature in their homes. Their bonsai represented Nature in miniature. A forest or a century old tree could be seen in the living room. For the same reason, years later, I built in my home small Asian gardens imitating nature in miniature with rocky hills and Koi pond with water lilies. Even in my retirement, I enjoyed life with nature at the beach, among the sand dunes and various attractive natural trails around the Bay Area. I felt lucky and fortunate to have learned at Lycée Yersin romanticism and Lamartine's "The Small Valley" poem leading me to the love of Nature for life. While in Dalat, on week-ends, I began to use my bike a lot to blend myself with Nature's beautiful lakes, hills and forest sites (see photos below)

During my three years in Da Lat I saw what nature had to offer as a source of consolation. As a result, my state of mental depression disappeared and this gave me the chance to concentrate on my studies. A picture is worth a thousand words. I have selected the following photos to describe my three years in Dalat, the Pearl of the Highlands in Vietnam:

Gougah Water Fall near Dalat 1951

Club House on the Lake

Club House Grenouillère for Swimmers

Couvent des Oiseaux : famous Catholic Girls School

Home like in a French city   *Old Chateau in downtown Da Lat*

Old Dalat Central Market 1951

Around this Central Market, it was a surprising fact for me to discover that in Dalat, like many other cities in Vietnam, the Chinese Vietnamese run most of the important businesses: groceries, restaurants and shops... No wonder they were called the "Jewish of the East."

Nguyễn Hữu Hào, Emperor Bảo Đại's father-in-law's Tomb

Nam Phương Hoàng Hậu Empress

Montagnard people. Highland Minority along the road

Highland Minority people along the road *Prenn Water Fall*

I frequently visited the farm regions surrounding Dalat, observing the different productions of the so called western vegetables and fruits. They were exported to Saigon and the Mekong Delta with its hot climate and strictly tropical produce.

Vegetable farm in Da Lat

Farming area with the famous Twin Lang Bian peaks in the background

Typical Western vegetable farms

Cut flowers and carrots from farm ready to be shipped to Saigon

Farm village

Dalat Western vegetables

Dalat Countryside

Lac des Soupirs

Protestant Church 1948

Saint Benoit Lake

Gougah Water Fall Dalat

Prenn Water Fall

Dalat Montagnard Women

Life after Lycée Yersin

When I finished my high school at Lycée Yersin Da Lat in 1951, the political situation in Vietnam was very bleak. The government had stopped issuing visas for students going abroad to study. Rumor was circulating around the town that there would be a mobilization for the war effort. By necessity and not by choice, I registered for premedical study because Vietnam did not have an Engineering school until 1957. Fortunately, the government announced that a teacher's job in junior high and up would be exempted from the draft because of urgent national need. With my valedictorian result in high school, I immediately got a job at my old Junior high school in Mỹ Tho, my Mekong Delta hometown (see photo below).

I was a member of the 1950-51 teaching staff of my Mỹ Tho Alma mater.
(First left of top standing row)

While teaching in Mỹ Tho, 70 km from Saigon, I had the luxury of using the family car, a French Peugeot 203, to visit the capital city on week-ends. My place of interest was USIS (United States Information Service), a US propaganda center. It was a modern public library, neat, well lighted place full of interesting magazines and books. The air conditioned, comfortable reading room reflected the high standard of living of the United States: lazy boys and chairs, functional design reading lamps, easy to find book card index. I was really impressed by the high standards of the USA.

One day, on the USIS bulletin board, I saw a flyer announcing scholarships for university education in America. Wow! For me it seemed like a miracle. Why? Because for Indochina (Cochinchina, Annam, Tonkin, Laos and Cambodia) the French created only one university in Hanoi without any Engineering school and my dream was to be an engineer. In the 50's, studying engineering in America was a prestige unheard of in Vietnam, a colony of France. There was no university in South Vietnam. Mrs. Bertha von Allmen from USIS, Saigon was processing my application. My greatest obstacle was how to convince her that I could study mechanical engineering in the US knowing only French and Vietnamese but with less fluency in English! I pointed out that my grades were very good in Math, Physics, Chemistry and Natural Sciences which were by themselves a universal language understood by people all over the world. Furthermore, the French language had also influenced English. Over nearly a thousand years, the English language had borrowed and absorbed a great number of French words and expressions though the English speakers might not be aware of their origins. During the Norman occupation, about 10,000 French words were mingled into English, some three-fourths of which are still in use in every domain, from government and law to art and literature as well as in science and technology. Mrs. von Allmen seemed to find my explanation reasonable and accepted my application.

To compete for this American scholarship, I was very hopeful thanks to my success as valedictorian at the Lycée Yersin. But besides the academic record, there were also background checks with three confidential letters from responsible parties. I was lucky to be able to find good people willing to help me. I went to two of my former school teachers, well known professors Võ Thanh Cứ and Lê Quang Nghĩa. Both knew me well for several years as a good student. They gladly took on my request to write the letters of recommendation to USIS in Saigon.

I wanted the signature of a great name on my third reference letter. Ngô Đình Thục was a catholic bishop. In the 30's he was a professor and Dean of the College of Providence in Huế, capital of Central Vietnam. He was later chosen by Rome to head the Apostolic Vicariate at Vĩnh Long, my parents' hometown. My Uncle Four, Dr. Khương Hữu Long, had a son study at Providence school in Huế and knew the bishop quite well. He was willing to ask the bishop to write a letter for me. With luck, I had all the help I could possibly get. All my hard work seemed to bear fruit and finally I got my scholarship. It was really the biggest, most unpredictable breakthrough, and one of the most important milestones of my journey ahead.

Ngô Đình Thục Bishop of Vĩnh Long

It was a miracle for me! Studying engineering in America was beyond the means of my family. After WWII, the U.S. had the best Engineering school in the world. But up to that time, almost all of the Vietnamese with their French secondary education would continue their engineering studies in France because their K-12 at a French Lycée in Vietnam was fully acceptable under the educational system in France and language was not a barrier for them as in my case going to America for higher education.

Up to then, everything seemed to progress smoothly toward my departure to the USA. Suddenly a huge road block stopped everything. I always thought that if I was fortunate to have earned a scholarship from the USIS agency, the government of Vietnam would issue a visa for my trip to America. It was unbelievable but true that the Interior ministry decided to refuse my exit visa. Why? I feel quite embarrassed to write down the rest of this story about my exit visa in 1951. It really hurt me, my people and my country. However, a life story should record both the good and the bad sides of events. It's a classic corruption case that shocked me brutally at the time. The Director of Cabinet of the Ministry of the Interior wanted some money for his signature on my exit visa! He happened to be one of the former well known teachers of my junior high school and was also considered a friend of my father. I often heard about corruption in the government but never expected it would affect me.

This was a crucial choice I had to make: pay for the visa signature to continue with my higher study or lose my American scholarship. Of course, the answer seemed obvious to me. But I felt a little reluctant to commit this act of corruption directly. A Good Samaritan came to my rescue. My father's next door neighbor "Thầy Bảy" (Mr. Bảy) happened to know this high official well. He volunteered to help me carry out the transaction!

How and where did I get the money? I had worked the previous 12 months as a teacher in my former junior high. The government payroll office was so slow that it took the whole year to issue my pay check of 26,000 VN piasters, the equivalent of US $715 then. I decided to sacrifice the whole year's salary for my future. I remember well taking the bus with Thầy Bảy from Mỹ Tho to Saigon and a taxi to Tân Định Church near the home of the corrupted official. I felt really bad having to play an active part in such a low-life action. Honestly and thank God that was the only time in my life.

As a Buddhist, I believe in the consequence of good and bad deeds. Many years later, in 1972, that despicable person came to see me in my Saigon office and asked for a job because he was unemployed. He really shocked me the second time for having the guts to see me again. I politely said that I had no job for him.

Well, that is what I am able to remember about that period in Da Lat and at the Lycée Yersin. It was a time of great challenge for a youngster in his late teens who was uprooted from his enjoyable childhood in a warm and loving family in the flat and tropical Mekong Delta to a far away French resort town high in the mountains with pine forests and the cold climate of the highlands. It was not only the sudden and abrupt change of the physical environment with profound homesickness and nostalgia but also the painful clash between his Vietnamese traditional values and the French way of life to which he had to comply in order to pursue his studies at the prestigious Lycée Yersin.

In fact, it was in this period at Da Lat and the Lycée Yersin that I was to discover the complex process of "East Meet West" and also to see the beginning of my very long and unbelievable journey in both time and space from one shore to the other of the vast Pacific Ocean, half the globe away. Dalat and the Lycée Yersin were the launching-pad and spring board of my maiden "Flight of the Eagle" to its predestination known as the New World.

Back to my story, the year 1952. Here I come, America!

PART 3

Learning the American Way

CHAPTER 6

**Immersion in Lafayette College
Pennsylvania, USA**

The Maiden Flight across the Pacific
My Very First Voyage by Plane, 1952

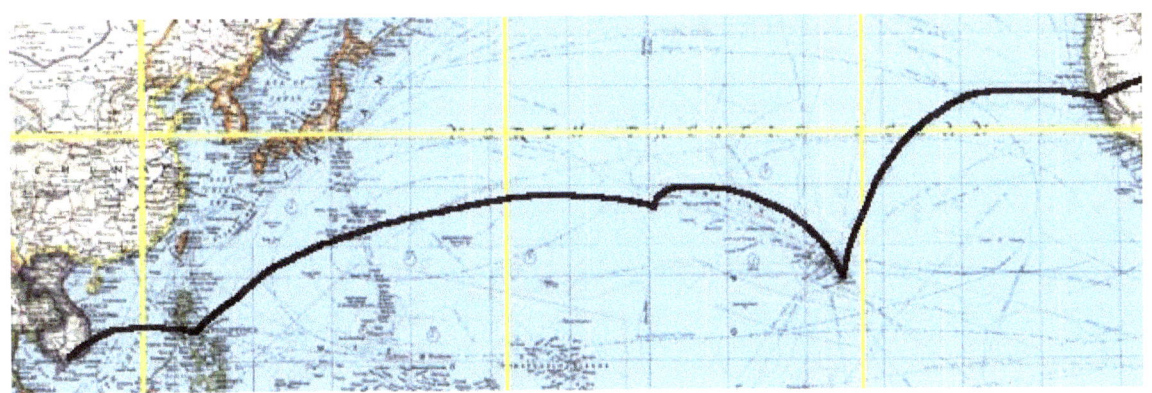

*Saigon-Manilla-Guam-Wake-Midway-Honolulu-San Francisco
by DC6-B*

It was my long journey to the American campus, a real frontal "EAST meets WEST." The choice of Lafayette College was not mine because I knew nothing about American universities and colleges. Almost all of the Vietnamese students continued their studies in France for the simple reason that since childhood they had followed the French colonial education system. In my case, I never had any course in English because it was not given in my junior high school with French as the first language and Vietnamese as the second.

The USIS (United States Information Service) Saigon office was processing my scholarship application for studying Mechanical Engineering in the U.S. Mrs. Bertha von Allman interviewed me in her Saigon USIS office on Hai Bà Trưng Street, near the famous French Grall Hospital. My academic requirement was more than adequate except for my big gap in English. I explained to Mrs. Allman that my math and sciences grades and my "Mention Bien" in French Baccalaureate in Mathematics would enable me to follow the engineering classes because math and sciences in themselves would be understood by people all over the world as universal languages. Besides, the English language had absorbed and been made up of more than 30% French words in it since its Norman times. I also promised to study English day and night to the day of my departure. Finally, like a miracle to me, I was granted a Fulbright scholarship to Lafayette College in Easton, Pennsylvania, a school selected by USIS. I was helped by Heaven to be sent to this relatively small school of about 2,000 students instead of larger universities with tens of thousands which would drown me in a big crowd especially with my very poor English.

For this problem, I bought immediately a 78 RPM "La Voix de Son Maitre" record player and Assimil vinyl disks with text books. I spent most of my time learning "My tailor is rich, my teacher is poor…" changing the steel needle of the phonograph and cranking by hand its spring for every face of the disk. I must admit now that my level of English was probably fit for a tourist but not for a first year Engineering student of any U.S. college. Mentally, in Saigon I envisaged a Total Immersion in English on the American campus without knowing the devastating consequences of that decision.

Châu, my classmate and I went shopping in Saigon to get ready for the long trip

For the first long trip to the New World, I selected the best I could have in my suitcase. In 1952, the French Grand Magasin Charner, GMC, was the best and biggest gallery in town. I found there the most modern light weight suitcase made in France. In those days, the maximum luggage for each passenger was only 20 kg compared to the 50 pounds allowed nowadays. My family gave me also the best camera in the family, a Rolleiflex, and an Omega watch.

The best suit and overcoat made with British wool and imported from Hong Kong were hand tailored by Mỹ Tho's top Hanoi Taylor. My mother wanted me to feel safe in difficult times alone overseas. She made sure that I had a ring mounted with a several carats diamond and a 24 carats heavy gold necklace. Of course, I always took great care of these valuable treasures by keeping them in a safe deposit box at the local bank.

Family friends made a special trip from Mỹ Tho to the Saigon Airport to send me off. As usual, Brother Five was always the good man and let me drive his small French Renault 4 CV to see for the last time my Lycée Yersin good friend at Laregnère Street. After parking, I forgot to turn off the car lights! When the time came to rush back home to go to the airport, the 4 CV car battery was dead. What a panicky moment! Fortunately, the 4 CV was a rather light car. My friend and I, we pushed it together then I jumped back inside to jump start the car by using the clutch. Thank God, the motor started and I did not miss the very important flight. What a catastrophe it would have been for me and my family if I got stuck in Saigon because of that incident. I later learned that my Yersin friend became professor of Mathematics at the famous French École Polytechnique and retired at Rue Xaintrailles in Paris.

I returned the Renault 4CV car to my brother Five, with my heart still beating heavily. There were many people waiting at the airport to see me off. I had experienced nostalgia and loneliness during previous departures to Dalat, only 400 km from Mỹ Tho with the knowledge that my return date was 10 months away. This time I would be separated from my family for at least 4 years and 14,000 km. Not a very comfortable thought. Probably the exceptional scholarship to the U.S. neutralized the pain of the moment. As the saying goes: live your life, one day at a time. "Que sera, sera." I did my best not to cry in front of my dear parents and relatives trying to convince myself that "the sadness of the departure was for those who stay behind." It was just a quick fix. Life was more complicated than that.

Saigon International Tân Sơn Nhứt Airport was so small that the terminal consisted of a modest single two-story building. The advantage was that the roof terrace was designed as a café bar for visitors. They could enjoy their drinks and waive their handkerchiefs to say good bye or to welcome home their friends and relatives, a dozen meters away. In the good old days, there was no danger from terrorists.

As a Mekong Delta boy, I was very excited to see the New World half way around the globe. It was also my very first voyage by plane. In the 50's, propeller planes could not make nonstop flight to the U.S. and the most direct itinerary was: Saigon Tân Sơn Nhứt airport to Manila, Guam, Wake, Midway Island, Honolulu, San Francisco, Pittsburgh, Harrisburg and finally the small regional airport Allentown-Bethlehem-Easton, Pennsylvania.

Saigon Tân Sơn Nhứt Airport 1952 *Pan Am hostess*

Our first time in the Famous Manila Hotel, put up by Pan Am due to a typhoon in the Pacific Ocean

At the Manila Hotel

    The chemistry that started in me when "East Met West" in Dalat for the first time was going to continue at a much more accelerated pace in a completely different environment and state of mind. After the maiden "Flight of the Eagle" from the shores of the Mekong Delta to San Francisco Bay, my life changed drastically. I left an underdeveloped French colony in Indochina and flew over the Pacific Ocean to study engineering in the most advanced country of the world in 1952. It was quite a big jump for a little guy. I would keep my eyes wide open to observe the new "black box or Pandora's Box." My stay at the Lycée Yersin had already instilled in me the essence of French good manners. Now I would be exposed to the new American way of life.

My initial Trans-Pacific journey, 8,880 miles (14,200 km) from the East to the West started with a typhoon in the Pacific Ocean. The propeller planes DC-6B and Constellation of this period could not fly above the bad weather like today's jets. As a result, the airline had to organize an unscheduled overnight stay at the famous Manila Hotel in the Philippines. The hotel was famous because it was the headquarters of General MacArthur during WWII. The trip itself was unique because the Pacific Ocean route was not ready for commercial aviation service. Many refueling stops were actually made at US Navy bases such as Wake and Midway islands in the Pacific where there were no civilian airports. The planes got refueled by the military personnel and the passengers took their meals at the Navy mess halls. It was a rare treat for me to know what life was like in the Navy. My adventure had really begun this way. I noted that in the early 50's, international flights were considered a luxury. Passengers were mostly well dressed. Airline seats were wide and comfortable unlike those in more modern times. Meals on planes were served with porcelain and silverware. No paper napkins, paper cups, plastic knifes and forks. Tourist class meant comfortable class. No messy security checks or strip searches at the airport like those in the 21st century. No shoes off either! It was very civilized, enjoyable travel. Another surprise in my life: I lived two Thursdays in one week on earth because I crossed the international dateline. Airline stewardess gave out souvenir certificates for the special occasion. For hours, I saw nothing but monotonous white clouds over the Ocean. Finally, the plane landed on American soil, Honolulu airport. I was very impressed by the exotic Hawaiian Hula dancers wearing colorful grass skirts and holding torches.

Hawaii Hula dance

Hawaii Hula dance

Torch fire dance

A new headache for me. The immigration papers must be completed at Honolulu airport before going to the mainland and I was not capable of filling them out in English. Fortunately for me there was TN Châu, my Yersin schoolmate, who happened to be on the same flight to America and he came to my rescue. He did all the required paperwork for me. Finally, the silhouette of the world famous Golden Gate Bridge appeared on the horizon announcing the arrival in the New World. I did not know then that this Golden Gate Bridge with its San Francisco Bay was to be many many years later the place for me to finally throw my anchor in the great American Nation.

Golden Gate Bridge

Arriving at San Francisco Airport Sept 1952

A First Hot Dog

My scholarship provided a few days of orientation in San Francisco to help me adjust to my new life in America. It was a very important moment in my life when East met West for the first time in a much more overwhelming way compared to my first experience at the little town of Dalat. It was the beginning of a long and very challenging journey. In San Francisco, the orientation program had Frank, a jovial American guide showing me what a newcomer should see in the Bay Area.

After the Golden Gate, I paid a visit to the Cliff House shop and restaurant. A mini shock happened when Frank offered me a "Hot Dog." Of course, in a Vietnamese village, some people could enjoy dog meat but I did not expect Americans to do that too! Not so, Frank told me that actually it was made with pork and beef. I learned later that the consumption of dog meat was found sometimes in Germany a long time ago. Therefore, the normal suspicion that sausages might have contained dog meat was occasionally justified. A hot dog can often be known under different names like frankfurter, frank, wiener, and weenie. Towards the end of the nineteenth century, clever students at Yale University in New Haven, Connecticut, began referring to sausages as dogs. A lunch wagon that operated there at night was called "The Kennel Club" because the hot dogs were its specialty with the sausage served in a bun garnished with mustard. Frank explained the origin of the word "dog" in the expression "Hot Dog" that way to convince me that there was no dog meat in the hot dogs in the U.S.. The term "dog" was used as a synonym of sausage already in 1884 and accusations of sausage-makers using dog meat had dated back to at least 1845.

The Cliff House, famous for its Rock full of seals

Old Cable Car

The Gate to Chinatown with the largest Chinese population outside of China and Taiwan

Union Square in the center of downtown & famous Saint Francis Hotel

The St. Francis became the hotel where Republican presidents stayed when in San Francisco.

Historic Fairmont

Democratic presidents usually stayed at the Fairmont. In 1945, the Fairmont hosted international statesmen for meetings which culminated in the creation of the United Nations. The United Nations Charter was drafted in the hotel's Garden Room and this major historical event was memorialized by a plaque at the hotel.

TWA, Constellation San Francisco-Pittsburgh-Easton, Pennsylvania

After a good time in San Francisco, I would be alone soon to continue my journey to Lafayette College, in Easton, Pennsylvania via Pittsburgh, Harrisburg, and finally Allentown-Bethlehem-Easton airports. There was no nonstop flight to the small town of Easton. This was a fascinating trip to the Lafayette College campus, all alone and this time without any help from my friend TN Châu with his fluency in English! I selected the window seat to observe the New World carefully. When the plane approached the airport at low altitude to prepare for landing, my first surprise was the millions of white chickens running freely on the many green farms. In Vietnam, we did not have any huge, mass production of chickens and eggs like that. I also saw giant, healthy weeping willow trees on those farms. In Vietnam, weeping willow was the symbol of the slim, slender, petite and graceful figure of a lady. What a contrast between East and West which had started with the "hot dog" in San Francisco!

At the airport, I felt relieved to have Mr. Lee, the Lafayette Director of foreign students, take care of my check-out and transportation to the campus. We stopped at Pardee Hall (see photo) to complete my registration as a freshman in engineering and to get a dormitory room in Easton Hall.

Pardee Hall, Lafayette College

Up to now, my journey was just one-week tourism. Now began the rough and tough academic *Immersion experience.*

Lithograph of Lafayette College, circa 1875

I had had a taste of immersion into the English language on the flight to the Pennsylvania campus, but now I was suddenly "thrown into the ocean to learn how to swim." No one spoke Vietnamese, or even French, so English was now my only option for communicating with the people around me. The feeling was not dissimilar to how I had felt when my father immersed me in the Mekong River to teach me how to swim. I choked in the murky water and lost my breath several times. Nowadays there are other more humane ways of teaching swimming but then - as now - I was scared to death, and had no choice but to learn how to stay above the water.

My registration at Pardee Hall, built in 1873

Easton Hall

Easton Hall, my dormitory, was built in 1926. My room was on the ground floor, on the other side of this façade, facing a small green forest.

Easton Hall Gate to downtown Easton

Lafayette Campus

Lafayette Campus in autumn

Campus in autumn

I will always remember those first few days at Lafayette. Coming from a war torn country, I was surprised to see so many century-old buildings around the campus, a clear sign that America had enjoyed peace for a long time through the course of its history. No such historic buildings could be found in South Vietnam due to the devastation of five decades of continuous wars following the nearly 100 years of French colonial rule.

My adventure of attending an American university began with getting to know my fellow freshman classmates in Easton Hall. They asked me where I came from, and when I told them Vietnam, they had no idea where that was! I reluctantly explained that Vietnam was formerly known as French Indochina, and only then did they seem to know it was somewhere in Asia. It seemed as if Americans were poorly versed in world geography. Even later, when I accepted invitations to speak to groups about Vietnam such as the Kiwanis and Rotary clubs, I was often asked the same questions. Once, at the Wilkes-Barres TV station, the staff provided me with photos of half naked montagnards, our Vietnamese equivalent to indigenous tribes living in the highland jungles, and referred to them as the "people of Vietnam!"

My next surprise was discovering that the dorm's shower facilities consisted of only one big room with six shower heads. No privacy at all; just everyone naked in the same room taking showers! It was quite a shock to me. With my long established Confucian upbringing, it had not even occurred to me that bathing would be a communal activity at my new school. Whereas I was eager to adapt myself to the American ways of life, I was not quite ready to strip down and forego my privacy. I would encounter a similar situation years later at Camp Pendleton, but for now my solution was to shower wearing swimming trunks.

My next door neighbor and freshman classmate was Don Sayenga, from Pittsburgh, Pennsylvania. He was over six feet tall and a heavyweight. I, on the other hand, was a five foot four, and a featherweight. Don belonged to the Lafayette football and wrestling teams. He was incredibly open hearted, and an incredibly nice guy. He did not intimidate or bully me with his physical superiority; on the contrary he seemed to protect me against adverse conditions on our floor. We became very close friends and our friendship has lasted over the years. With Don's help, I endured many surprises as I found ways to adapt to being a "stranger in a strange land."

Don Sayenga came to see me in California after my camp Pendleton time, 1975

Among the many surprises that I encountered, one of the biggest was the food. Everything about it was completely different. As soon as I arrived in America, I had to switch completely from chopsticks to knife and forks, from rice to cereals and bread, and from water to milk. Since Vietnam had no dairy industry, I had never had fresh milk. I had only the expensive, imported sweet and condensed milk that we added to our black coffee. Furthermore, as if I didn't stand out enough as a small Asian fellow speaking broken English, I discovered that my hand tailored shirts and trousers further singled me out as a newly arrived foreigner on campus. I quickly traded them in for blue jeans, T-shirts, and a warm jacket to blend into the crowd.

My math, physics and chemistry classes were smooth sailing, but I had to drop my surveying class because the colonel teaching the course had a very strong and incomprehensible accent from Alabama. Instead I took a speed reading class, and English for foreigners. The first few weeks around the campus were so intense that I lost track of time and my brain was so full that there was no room for feeling nostalgic or homesick. Then suddenly, I felt like I had been struck by lightning when I received a letter from the Institute of International Education in New York that was administering my scholarship. It stated that my program was good only for one year and it was not renewable. What a shock! My parents could not possibly afford thousands of dollars to finance my next three years of college, and I couldn't bear the thought of going home without a degree. I couldn't understand why USIS in Saigon had not told me this in advance. Was it my fate, my destiny? Had I known this beforehand I probably would have given up on my dream of studying in America.

I carefully read the letter again and was able to find a loop hole, a silver lining. The fine print mentioned that they would help me renew my student visa if I could prove that I could support myself next year. After some brainstorming with friends, I came up with a solution. I would save most of my existing scholarship money for next year, and look for every possible way to work for food or cash. I was sure that I could make it work by limiting my expenses to a bare minimum. This kind of challenge hardened my character, made a man out of the boy inside me. In retrospect, the fear of failure was so great that all the painful sacrifices seemed small, and this unprecedented period of survival had a direct influence on my future achievements and success in life. And so, in this way I received a baptism of fire right there on campus. Frank R. Hunt, the dean of students, became my first American Good Samaritan. He and Mrs. Hunt lived in a small villa on 3 West Campus in Easton. He offered me a small room near his kitchen for free, so that I might be able to continue my studies. In return, I would help with little jobs like washing the car, cutting the grass, and sweeping the fallen leaves in the yard.

Dean Hunt's home where I lived from 1953 to 1956

Dean Hunt's home

On the Hunt's front lawn with my twin from Paris; graduation day May 1956

I also found a job as a dishwasher and/or waiter in Watson Hall, a student residence with in-house eating facilities. The management of Watson Hall and its residents was done by the students themselves, with the help of the housemaster, who also lived at the hall. In this case, Dr. Saalfrank, the head of the Mathematics Department, served as the housemaster. The only person hired from off campus was the full time professional cook.

Watson Hall Student Residence, a gift from IBM

By working two hours a day, I got my breakfast, lunch and dinner for free. For a Vietnamese from a well-off middle class family, having to wash dishes or wait on tables was surely unheard of. Asians looked upon manual labor as degrading. But I saw it as "other lands, other customs." Apparently, even the son of Pennsylvania's governor did manual work on the highway projects. I remember how reluctant I was to put on my white waiter's uniform to serve boys and girls in the Watson Hall dining room; but the dye was cast and on the first day of work, several of my coworkers opened the kitchen door and launched me out to "sea" like a boat! I continued to work for my meals for the next three and a half years. There were no tips. Once in a while I was invited to eat at the table where French was spoken to help students practice the language. On those days I did not wait on tables or wash dishes, even for my own meals. Actually, washing dishes by machine was an easy task. The machine did all the washing, rinsing and drying. I just put dirty dishes on the tray, let the machine do its thing, and took out the clean dishes when it was done. I also had another waiter job on campus at the Hogg Hall cafeteria, where I mostly waited on tables, but also learned how to grill hamburgers and hot dogs. With this job I earned the minimum wage of one dollar per hour, but also received tips. Students were not good tippers however, and during the entire period between 1952 and 1956, I never got a tip of more than a quarter. Nowadays, I always leave good tips to waiters, having been in their shoes before.

Around the campus many professors had their houses cleaned by students, and Dr. Pascal, a French teacher, hired me to keep his heater filled with coal. In the 50's, many homes in Pennsylvania were heated by gravity-fed coal burning heaters installed in the basement. Trucks on the street level would fill up the heaters or coal hoppers in the basement with granular coal through a big pipe. A huge inverted pyramid funnel installed on the top of the heaters received the coal. I was hired to go down to the dark, cold basement to refill the coal funnel by hand. I remember covering my nose with a handkerchief which of course, was white in those days. By the time I finished the job my handkerchief would be completely black around my nose. For this miserable job, I was still only paid one dollar per hour. Nevertheless the value of those dollars strengthened my character. Looking back now, I think I would hesitate to repeat the same experience, but not all of my jobs were so difficult or dirty. For example my former math teachers let me grade their students' quizzes which were given every few weeks.

On week-ends, some professors hired students to help collect scientific data in the lab for their research papers. I quickly began to realize that many students in America "worked their way through college," a normal, laudable and honorable practice - nothing to be ashamed of, as it would be in the East. My biggest problem, however, was time. It was a constant balancing act between work and studies. My first two years proved to be the most challenging. I had to spend countless hours doing homework for my engineering courses, all the while working to earn enough money for the renewal of my student visa for the following year.

Nowadays, looking back more than half century ago, I cannot help but feel both awed and somewhat overwhelmed by the progress that the world has made in both science and engineering. Back in the 50's when I was in school, engineering students used long bamboo slide rules. There were no personal computers, pocket calculators, iPads or tablets. The slide rule was used for multiplication and division, plus functions such as roots, logarithms and trigonometry. Everyday on the campus, engineering students walked from class to class with a 10-inch leather slide rule case hooked to their belt like a weapon. The use of slide rules continued to grow through the 1950's and 1960's, but by the early 70's, the electronic calculator made the slide rule largely obsolete.

Engineering was more difficult for me than for my American classmates. This was most probably because they had grown up in a more mechanized society than I did. In America, it was common for teenagers to drive and maintain their own cars, which was rare in the East. Similarly, many students were already familiar with farm machinery and other mechanical gadgets. It was obvious that this hands-on experience gave them a clear advantage in their lab work. I did my best to breach the knowledge gap between myself and classmates by visiting as many manufacturing plants as possible.

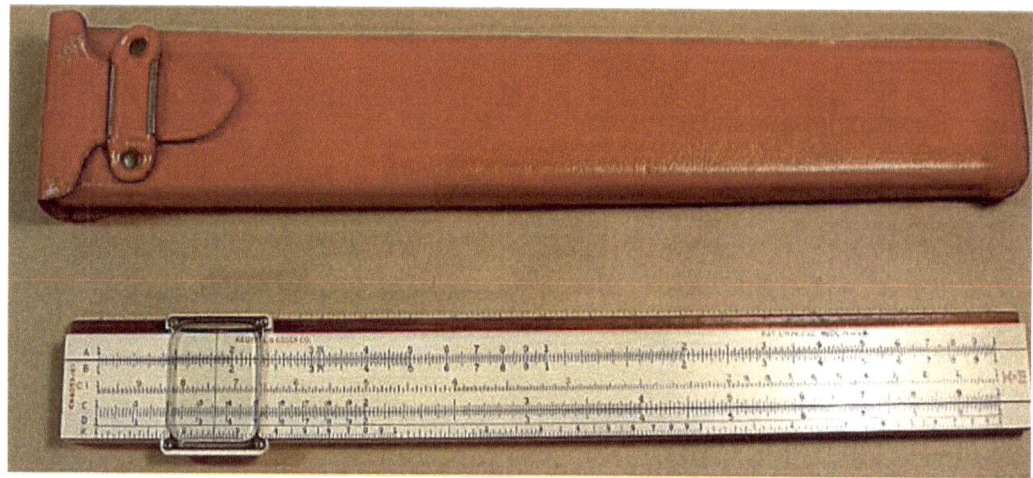
Standard 10-inch slide rule with leather case

Preston and Điểu doing homework, Easton Hall 1953

Money wasn't the only reason that I pushed myself to apply for a tuition scholarship for the following year. I also needed good grades. In addition to passing the dreadful English classes, I had to make sure that I got high marks in mathematics, physics and chemistry. The American academic system was completely different from what I was used to, but I grew to appreciate the differences. For one, the relationship between students and professors was quite informal, and there was a constant flow of liberal exchange between them. Secondly, in contrast to Vietnam where the students took only the final exams at the end of the year to pass the course, the American system was based on quizzes all year round. I liked this new test approach since it allowed me to spread my study load more evenly over time, rather than cramming intensely for just the final exams. I also appreciated the honor system observed by the college because it showed respect for the students, who were forced to feel responsible for their own deeds.

Tau Beta Pi, *Standing:* Stantz, Wild, Fellin, and Herring; *Sitting:* Dieli, Goldberg, Burcak, Gehman, Layden, Shinal, and Shotwell, is the honorary engineering fraternity which recognizes scholarship and campus participation among the engineers.

I experienced a very difficult beginning at Lafayette, however, like a piece of soft iron being crafted into a fine sword, I became harder and sharper in dealing with problems. Admittedly, at times I felt terribly homesick, with my beloved family seemingly a million miles away. I can remember looking through my window in Easton Hall crying quietly on many a rainy night, but I was willing to pay the price of a few tears in order to gain financial viability and to overcome the fear of failure. I realized that there was nothing degrading about doing manual labor or even waiting on tables. Each time I found a dime or a quarter left on the table, I felt it was fair for the work I did - not charity dispensed by my fellow students at Lafayette. I learned to appreciate the real value of money, knowing that it had come from my own sweat and sacrifice. It was a memorable lesson on financial independence and how to live within my means, a useful tool that has served me well - especially during retirement.

During my years at Lafayette, I discovered another soothing treasure - classical music. In high school, I had learned from the poet, Lamartine, how nature could serve as a source of consolation. Now I found that classical music could do the same. During my school days in Vietnam, I had never been exposed to the works of Beethoven, Mozart, Dvorack, Tchaikovsky and others, but now the world of classical music opened up to me, and I took solace in its ability to uplift my spirit and smooth my soul. Later, when I returned to Vietnam, I shipped home several hundred long playing records and a good hi-fi system - my most treasured souvenir from America.

Summer work:

During summer, I kept myself busy working to save money for the renewal of my student visa. I enjoyed my job as a counselor in summer camps in Naples, Maine, teaching swimming to the boys and making field trips to New Hampshire mountains.

Camp counselor in New Hampshire; swimming instructor, Naples, Maine 1953

Another summer, I stayed on the campus doing lab work in sand casting to collect data for Dr. William Childs's foundry research paper.

Social life:

Around the campus, there were many church organizations whose members sponsored foreign students to help them familiarize with the American way of life and to make them feel less lonely in a new land. I was lucky to be introduced to the Miller family in 1953 by the downtown Presbyterian Church. I became a member of the family ever since. During the holidays they took me to various parts of the country: the Hershey's Chocolate World in Hershey, PA, an entertainment complex which also includes Hersheypark. We visited the Jersey shores, the Pocono Mountains, the Delaware Water Gap National Recreation Area and New York City which is only 70 miles away.

Week-end at the Miller's home 1953

Weekend at Joan Flagler's home

Bud Miller visit Saigon 1967

Friend in Florida trip with Dean & Mrs Hunt; Touring NYC with schoolmates

Trip to Florida with Dean& Mrs Hunt; Social life at Rutgers University 1956

Christmas 1953, Rockefeller Plaza in New York City

I met two friends from Vietnam: Chẩn working for VOA New York and Mr. Mô, Saigon Postmaster in mission here.

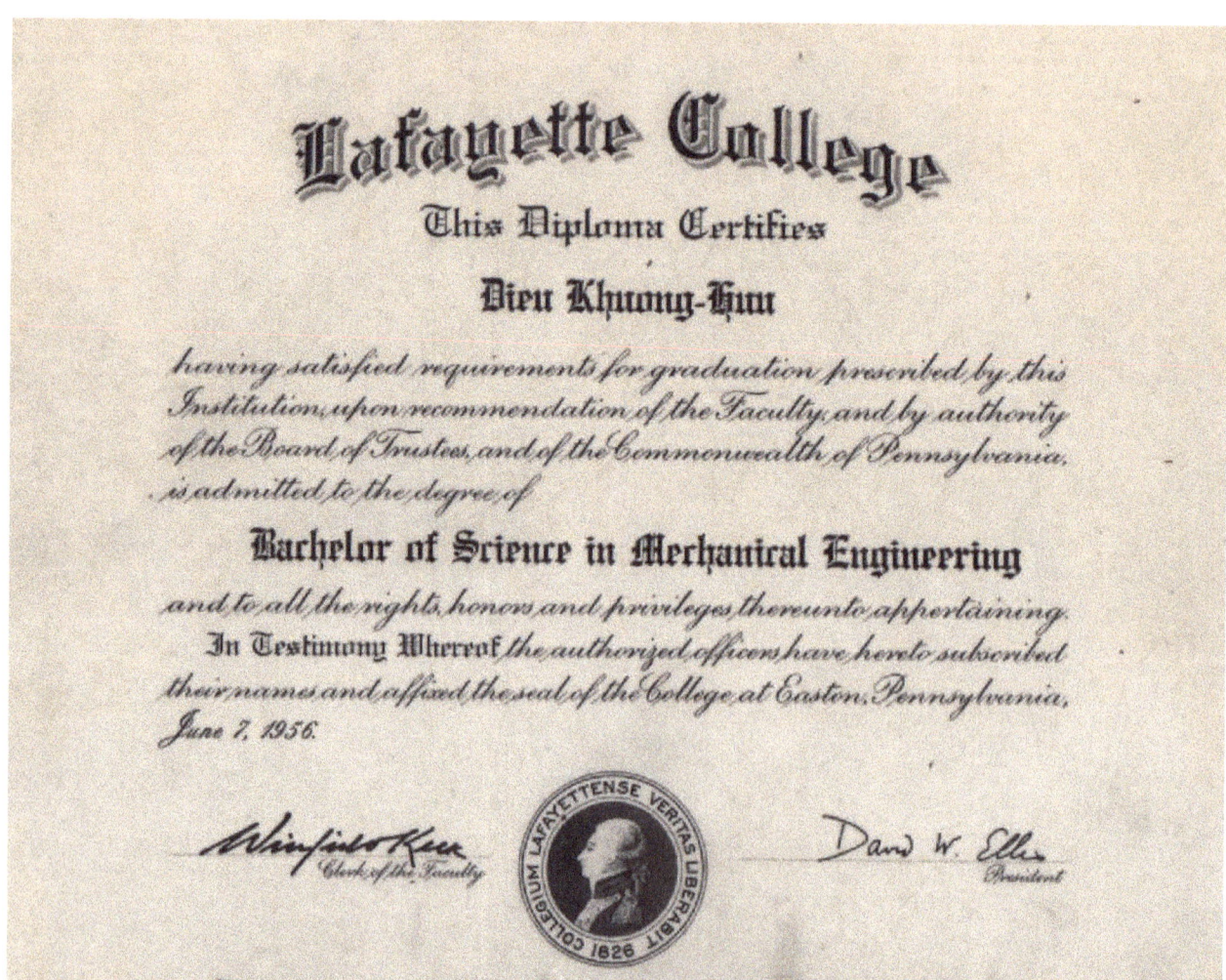

Looking back at my first encounter when "EAST meets WEST" at the Lycée Yersin, the clash was relatively a minor one compared to what I had to deal with at Lafayette College. My struggle with French manners in Dalat took place when I still lived in my country and was surrounded by my familiar Vietnamese environment with its traditions and customs. I was then a young man from a well-to-do family having comfortable living conditions and the joy of seeing occasionally my parents and relatives. At Lafayette College, I was completely submerged in the American way of life and had to work as a waiter and handyman for my room and board to see me through college. Lafayette College was my first real battle when "EAST meets WEST" right on the American soil and it was only the beginning. Many more battles and much greater challenges were awaiting me at the prestigious MIT in Boston, Massachusetts...

CHAPTER 7

Challenge at MIT

Survival of the fittest!

The summer of 1956 marked the most challenging milestone of my academic life. During my senior year at Lafayette College in Pennsylvania, I had applied for fellowship from the Ivy League schools and participated in the Tau Beta Pi (Engineering Honorary Society) competition for financial assistance. The title of the essay contest was "The role of Union and Management in a corporation."

The unexpected breaking news appeared in The New York Times Sunday June 3, 1956. (see insert) It announced my winning one of the five US Fellowships from Tau Beta Pi to study at MIT for a Master's degree in Mechanical Engineering.

Tau Beta Pi
"Tau Beta Pi was founded in 1885 to mark in a fitting manner those who have conferred honor upon their alma mater by distinguished scholarship and exemplary character as undergraduates in the field of engineering, or by their attainments as alumni in the field of engineering, and to foster a spirit of liberal culture in the engineering colleges."

The New York Times
Sunday, June 3, 1956

Sunday June 3, 1956
"Special to the New York Times."
EASTON, Pa. June 2

"A Vietnamese student at Lafayette College has won a fellowship to Massachusetts Institute of Technology, the college said last week. He is Dieu Huu Khuong, a senior. He ranks first in his field of study, although he has had to work his way through college. He will receive a Bachelor of Science degree in mechanical engineering at Lafayette's commencement Thursday. He won one of the five Tau Beta Pi Association fellowships. It will enable him to study at M.I.T. for a Master's degree in mechanical engineering. After that he plans to return to Vietnam to work there."
The Easton Express
JUNE 2, 1956

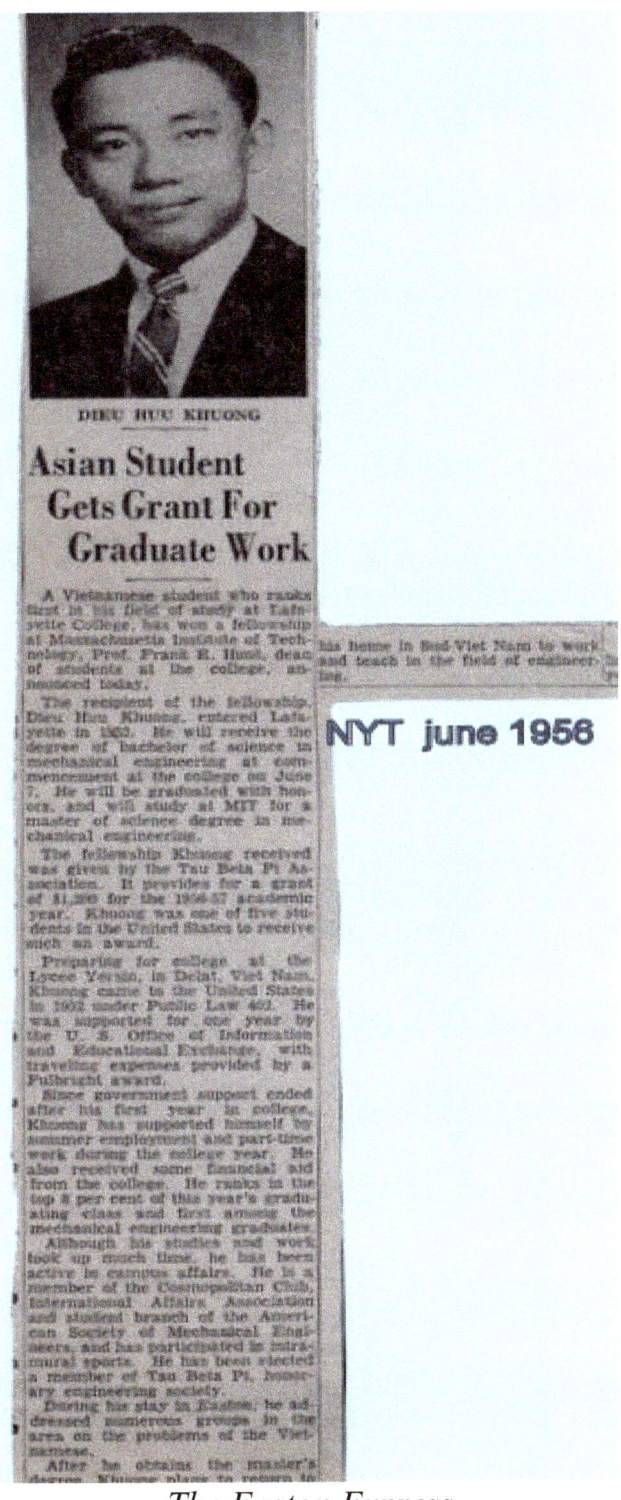

The Easton Express
Easton, PA - June 2, 1956
"Asian Student Gets Grant for Graduate Work"

"A Vietnamese student, who ranks first in the field of his study at Lafayette College, has won a fellowship at Massachusetts Institute of Technology, Prof. Frank R. Hunt, dean of students at the college, announced today.

The recipient of the fellowship Dieu Huu Khuong entered Lafayette in 1952. He will receive a degree of Bachelor of Science in mechanical engineering at commencement of the college on June 7. He will be graduated with honor, and will study at MIT for a Master of Science degree in mechanical engineering. The fellowship Khuong received was given by Tau Beta Pi Association. It provided for a grant of $1200 for the 1956-57 academic year. Khuong was one of five students in the United States to receive such an award.

Preparing for college at the Lycee Yersin, in Dalat, Viet Nam, Khuong came to the United States in 1952 under public Law 402. He was supported for one year by the U.S. Office of Information and Educational Exchange, with traveling expenses provided by a Fulbright award. Since government support ended after his first year in college, Khuong has supported himself by summer employment and part-time work during the college year. He also received some financial aid from the college. He ranks in the top 8 per cent of this year's graduating class and first among the mechanical engineering graduates. Although his studies and work took up much time, he has been active in campus affairs. He is a member of the Cosmopolitan Club, International Affairs Association and student branch of the American Society of Mechanical Engineering, and has participated in intra mural sports. He has been elected a member of Tau Beta Pi, honorary engineering society. During his stay in Easton, he addressed numerous groups in the area on the problems of the Vietnamese.

After he obtained the Master's degree, Khuong plans to return to his home in Sud-Viet Nam to work and teach in the field of engineering."

2011, MIT 150th anniversary

Concurrently, I had fellowship offers from Cornell, Columbia, Yale, Michigan State and Princeton universities for graduate work. To be fair to other graduate student applicants, I immediately sent telegrams to the above schools to thank them but stating I could not accept their rewards.

It was one of the happiest moments of my life because, not that much earlier I had started with great difficulty the undergraduate study through Immersion in English in Pennsylvania. Starting my study in the US with only my baggage of French and Vietnamese languages was the scariest experiment. Of course, the greatest reward was finishing first in Mechanical Engineering class leading to the fellowship for my graduate study at MIT. Truly, *America was the Land of Opportunity*. The tough part of my undergraduate life was over. Thank God, with a full fellowship, I did not have to do non-school work to meet my financial needs but could devote full time and energy to study.

Right after receiving my "sheep skin" (in my days, a diploma was really made of sheep skin, not paper) from the hand of Vice President Richard Nixon, the commencement speaker at Lafayette College, I moved immediately to the MIT campus in Cambridge via the Pennsylvania Railroad. I did not waste any time for my next objective. With a new invigorating gung-ho spirit, I had to finish my Master's degree on schedule fixed by the donor organization. The most efficient and pragmatic solution was to check in right away at the MIT campus Graduate House. No time should be wasted searching for a decent room in the new city. I shared a room with two American graduate students, Bauer and Wilson. The camaraderie was a placebo for loneliness.

My first question was why and how this school became so challenging and so hard to get accepted to become one of its student? Because MIT graduates were among the highest earners among all colleges and engineering schools. Also, according to the Institute, 76 "present and former members of the MIT community had won the Nobel Prize." I was very worried and felt intimidated by the school's reputation. A lack of self confidence and an inferiority complex started to build up in my sub conscience. What If I failed? What if I could not finish on schedule? The fear of failure made many of my demanding sacrifices less painful. I had to speed up my orientation and integration into the new campus life, and learned a lot from the old timers.

The first impression of the campus was very gratifying. From the window of my room in the Graduate house, (photo below) I saw two modern buildings across the street: The Kresge Auditorium and the MIT chapel.

The Graduate House

My room was on the third floor on the other side of this façade

The Kresge Auditorium

The Kresge Auditorium

The sight was striking with the elegant thin shell structure of reinforced concrete, one-eighth of a sphere, sliced away by sheer glass curtain walls so that it could come to earth at only three small points. Thin shell technology was innovative for the times. It was designed by noted Finnish architect Eero Saarinen and dedicated in 1955. Saarinen designed it in tandem with his MIT Chapel.

The two buildings were separated by a "green," referred to by students as the "Kresge Oval."

The MIT chapel

This MIT Chapel was a non-denominational chapel

The white marble altar was designed for multi-religion services. It could be lowered, rearranged and redecorated for the next religious service. The ensemble was recognized as one of the best examples of <u>mid-Century modern</u> architecture in the US.

Stata Center for Computer, Information, and Intelligence Sciences

Simmons Hall

Some of the buildings were just absolutely awesome (the Dome in particular was a terrific sight on a beautiful day, especially across from Memorial Drive). Some of them were weird: Simmons, Stata, (See photos.) But at least they kept them interesting and we did not have boring little red brick buildings that are all indistinguishable from each other.

What were the academics like at MIT?

The best thing about MIT was probably the academics. An education at MIT could easily be considered one of the most intense and rewarding of any institution in the world. The classes here were all tough, and it was a new experience for a lot of students. They may be used to receive all A's in their previous schools but now at MIT the A ratings could no longer be achieved easily. The results were suddenly about 50% lower in exams on subjects they had been quite familiar with. Like everybody else, I learned to adapt myself to the MIT standards and the academics pushed me to reach my higher potentials. Everyone was smart, and the jokes they told required a high baseline of knowledge, but it was fun. The most frequent student complaints were about the lack of sleep from working all night on problem sets. Although there were a lot of really smart students at MIT, most students were garden-variety smart and hard-working. You definitely had to be smart to get into MIT, but you didn't need to be some sort of otherworldly genius.

While I was in Vietnam, my obsession was to study at the famous Paris Grandes Écoles (Polytechnique, École Centrale, Supelec, HEC [Hautes Études Commerciales], ENA [Ecole Nationale d'Administration, ENS [École Normale Supérieure] and the Écoles des Mines,) whose Alumni ran France's government and practically most of the great corporations and agencies of France and Viet Nam. In the Grandes Écoles of France, the competition was very great but only among French or former French Empire students. They were national institutions for higher education in France.

MIT was a global institution. I had to compete with the top students of the whole world. This perception alone continued to bother me a lot. It forced me to be all I could to survive. By analogy, I put myself in the competitive mode of athletes in the Olympic Games during my academic years at MIT. Thank God, with the full fellowship, there was no non-school work to be done to meet my financial needs. But here again, I felt like a tennis champion in a local club going to the challenge of the prestigious US Open! The first contact with MIT academics was my registration and selection of courses in the Department of Mechanical Engineering called Course 2. MIT students referred to both their majors and classes using numbers or acronyms alone. Departments and their corresponding majors were numbered in the approximate order of their foundation; for example, Civil and Environmental Engineering was Course I, while Nuclear Science & Engineering was Course XXII. Students majoring in Electrical Engineering and Computer Science, the most popular department, collectively identified themselves as "Course VI." MIT students used a combination of the department's course number and the number assigned to the class to identify their subjects; the course which many American universities would designate as "Physics 101" was, at MIT, simply "8.01."

I was looking for courses adapted to the needs of Vietnam, a developing country. For instance, they were Ventilating and Air Conditioning, Refrigeration, Internal Combustion Engines, Foundry…To my big surprise, I was told that those courses were no longer taught at MIT. The lab had just removed the equipment of those conventional courses and replaced them with high tech supersonic wind tunnel, shock tubes, etc…I had to select the new high-tech courses for my degree. I had to learn the high-tech thinking process rather than taking conventional courses. I asked myself how to get out of this place on time.

For Mechanical Engineering, it was a privilege to study Advanced Thermodynamics with Professor Joseph H. Keenan, world famous for his textbooks on Thermodynamics, Gas and Steam Tables. They had been used extensively in design and engineering work related to jet and rocket propulsion and gas turbines. He was a very popular teacher. Our class had even a chance to be invited to his home. His home office desk was surrounded by nothing but the four white wall bookshelves. I was surprised to learn that he earned only a bachelor's degree in naval architecture and marine engineering at the Massachusetts Institute of Technology in 1922. Most Department heads had their Ph. D. or Sc. D. Only a genius deserved exception.

My next course was advanced Refrigeration, Cryogenics with Professor Samuel C. Collins, internationally known as the father of practical helium liquefiers and founder of the MIT Cryogenic Engineering Laboratory. During WWII, Dr. Collins developed an airborne oxygen generator for the flying fortresses, producing high purity oxygen. He was also known for developing - in collaboration with a surgeon at the Veterans Hospital in West Roxbury, a suburb of Boston - a compact heart-lung machine. The device, completed in 1964, was small enough to fit into the trunk of a car.

My academic adviser helped me fulfill my Master's Degree requirements with turbo machinery, advanced metallurgy, hydro power, and pumped storage courses. The thesis work was on flame stability at a supersonic speed. With the academic program approved for Course 2, my next step appeared very clear. It would be again 10% inspiration and 90% perspiration. I had done this once in Pennsylvania via *IMMERSION*. This time I was convinced that the same hard work with passion, persistence and patience would carry me through the rough time. My classmates did their homework with a typewriter. During all my student life, I had to use my hand writing only. It was the same way for all the students in Vietnam. With my thesis work, the Department took care of my typing with the help of a very competent secretary, Loulou Bernier. There were some pleasant moments to discuss thesis project work with her at the Du Barry French restaurant across the Charles River.

With my thesis assistant Loulou Bernier, MIT1957

The tense moment for my final exam was at last over with my Master's thesis approved by Professor White, my supervisor. I was told by Department 2 that I met all the requirements for my graduation. Thank God. What a relief to take a good deep breath and wait for the great day. It would be the end of my formal academic life after 17 years of sweat, tears and joy.

Graduation Day Loneliness

Graduation day at MIT

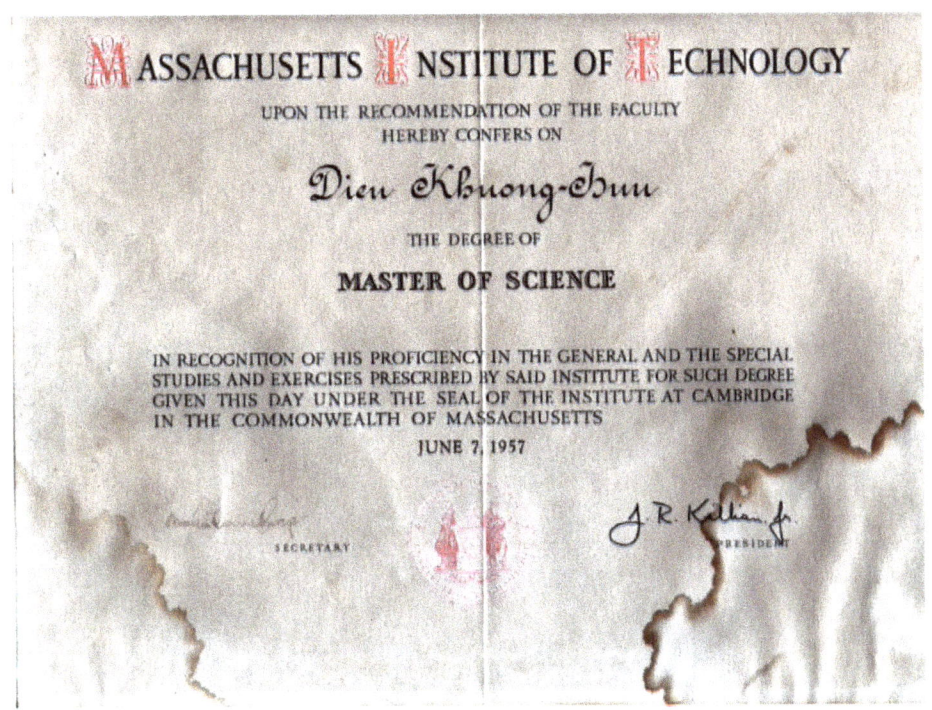

Normally, graduation should be a joyful celebration day. Unfortunately, it was one of the loneliest days of my seven years away from home. Among the joyful crowd, I just sat there impassive in the open air space, in front of the Killian Court Dome in the midst of cheerful future graduates wearing our black uniforms. I could not find any relative or longtime friend to join me and share this greatest day of my academic life. Thousands of students were whooping and hollering and generally having a great time. Everyone but me who was sad, very sad. To me, feeling so lonely at such an outstanding event, nothing about this graduation ceremony seemed celebratory. I sat there lonely among the big crowd waiting impatiently for my turn to pick up the diploma. Then I went back to my room not to join any joyful party but to pack up for my trip to New York City and begin my new job there.

But being an optimist, there was no time for me to cry on this special occasion. Quickly, I was able to turn my thoughts to something more positive: cheers instead of tears! When I was at the French Lycée Yersin in Dalat, I always had a dream to someday graduate from the most prestigious school in France: École Polytechnique de Paris. Now, fortunately my dream did come true even better than what I had hoped for. From the recent information given by the École Polytechnique itself, this French school ranks 36th in the world classification while MIT tops the list as first. Furthermore, after WWII, English had gradually emerged as the international language in this increasingly competitive world. After Lafayette College and MIT, not only did I learn Mechanical Engineering but also acquired a solid knowledge of English. If I were from Polytechnique de Paris, French would not have been as useful and helpful for my professional activities and career both in Vietnam and later during the following 40 years of my life in America.

QS World University Rankings® 2012/17
The best universities in the world

Institution	2012/13	2013/14	2014/15	2015/16	2016/17
Massachusetts Institute of Technology	1	1	1	1	1
Harvard University	3	2	4	2	3
Stanford University	15	7	7	3	2
University of Cambridge	2	3	2	3	4
California Institute of Technology	10	10	8	5	5
University of Oxford	5	6	5	6	6
University College London	4	4	5	7	7
Imperial College London	6	5	2	8	9
Ecole Normale Supérieure	34	28	24	23	33

Institution	2012/13	2013/14	2014/15	2015/16	2016/17
Seoul National University	37	35	31	36	35
University of Bristol	28	30	29	37	41
Kyoto University	35	35	36	38	37
The University of Tokyo	30	32	31	39	34
Ecole Polytechnique	41	41	35	40	53

Nobel Prize Winners By Country		
Rank	*Country*	*Nobel Prizes*
1	United States	353
2	United Kingdom	125
3	Germany	105
4	France	61

Office of the Provost: Nobel prize at MIT: 85

As of 2015, 52 National Medal of Science recipients, 65 Marshall Scholars, 45 Rhodes Scholars, 38 MacArthur Fellows, 34 astronauts, 19 Turing award winners, 16 Chief Scientists of the U.S. Air Force and 6 Fields Medalists have been affiliated with MIT. The school has a strong entrepreneurial culture, and the aggregated revenues of companies founded by MIT alumni would rank as the eleventh-largest economy in the world.

Why Is MIT So Strong?

A very strong budget

Operating Expenditures
(in Millions)*

Fiscal Year 2015

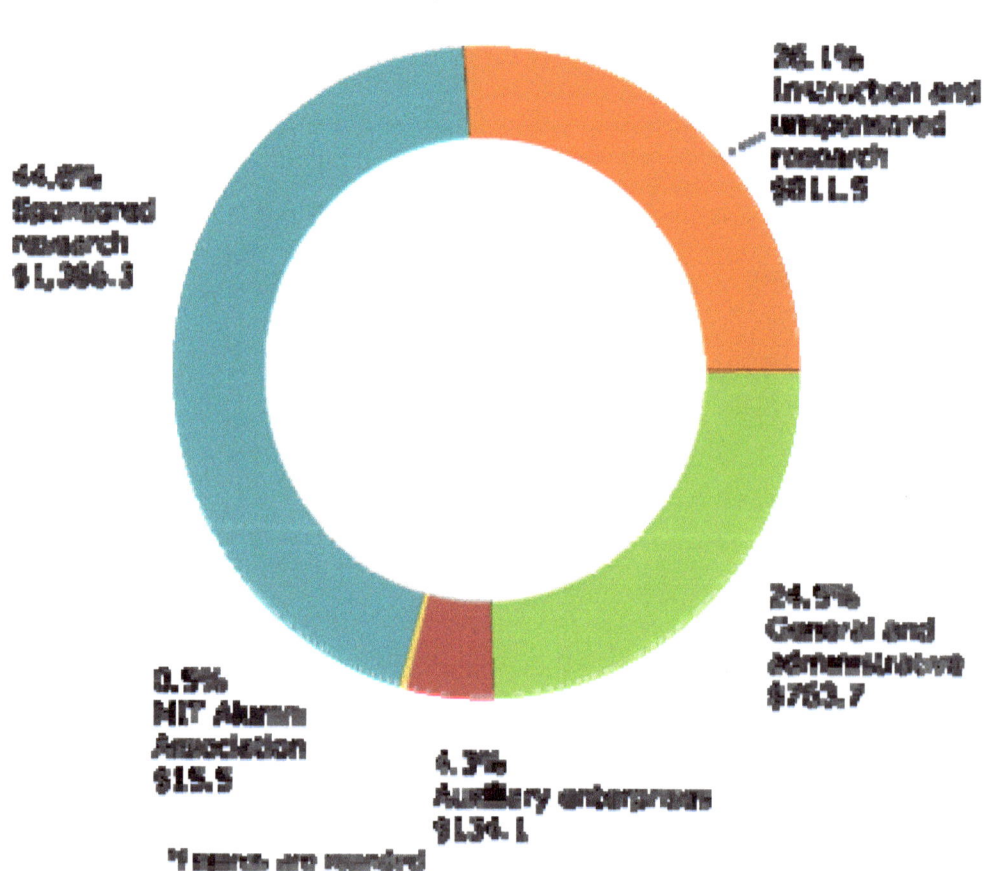

The budget for research is more than 2 billions dollars a year!

Operating Revenues
(in Millions)*
Fiscal Year 2015
Total: $3,290.8

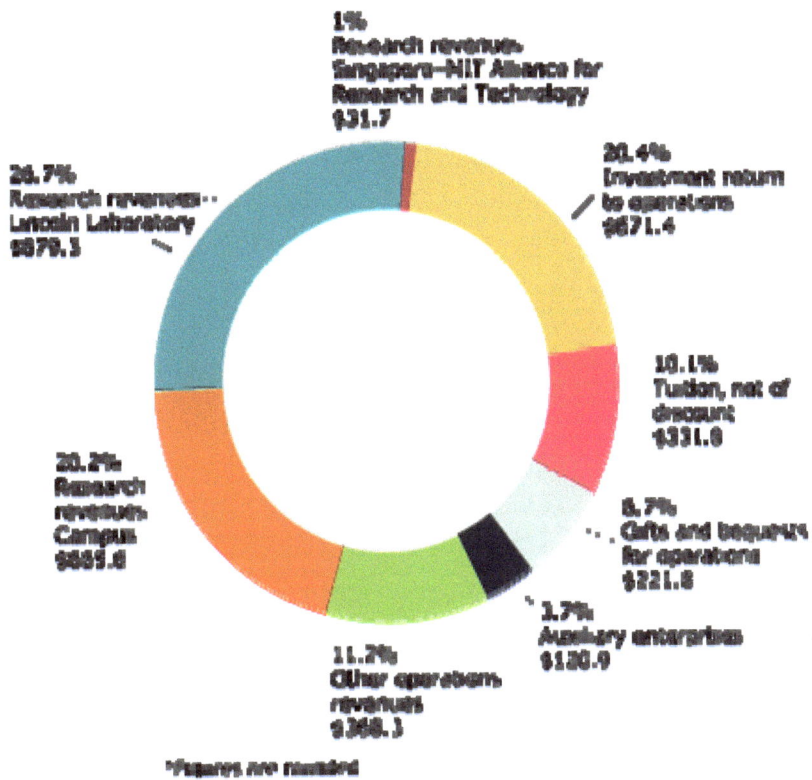

Research revenues more than 1.5 billions dollars a year!

Reminiscing about my MIT years some six decades ago, I cannot refrain from finding out how my old school has now become the world #1. Currently, over 700 companies are working with MIT faculty and students both in Institute-wide programs or in smaller collaborations. Among these corporate sponsors are such global leaders as BAE, BP, Du Pont, ENI, Ford Motor, Google, Intel, Lockheed Martin, Novartis, Quanta Computer, Raytheon, Samsung, Sanofi, Shell, Siemens, and TOTAL… Research sponsored directly by industry totaled $133 million in fiscal year 2012, or 20 percent of all MIT research funding. According to the National Science Foundation, MIT ranks first in industry-financed research and development and development expenditures among all universities and colleges. This great name school with the largest fund for research and development obviously attracts the best talents of the world. "The rich gets richer" and the strong gets stronger. I feel proud of my school to know that, in my life time, I saw many talented alumni such as Kofi Annan, Benjamin Netanyahu, Ben Bernanke, Alfred Sloan, Paul Krugman, Joseph Stiglitz, George Shultz, Mario Draghi, Nicholas Negroponte, IM Pei, Lawrence Summers, John Sununu…

Summary of Academic Journey

Indeed, MIT was an important landmark in my life. The completion of the post-graduate master's degree in Mechanical Engineering there also marked the end of my student days and academic life. At the time in the 1950s, it was also the greatest challenge and achievement for the schoolboy from Mỹ Tho, in the faraway Mekong Delta.

That evening after my graduation ceremony, I sat alone in my room and tried to understand what just had happened to me. All kinds of memories flashed back to my mind. My thoughts first went to my beloved parents, siblings, relatives and friends in Mỹ Tho, my childhood days in the Mekong Delta, and the very long journey from one school to another and eventually to the graduation at MIT. Many people had told me that their student days were the best times of their lives. It was also true in a way for me, a little boy from the Mekong Delta, growing up under French colonial rule but fortunate enough to be in a well-to-do family with hard working parents in successful business activities. They did try to give me the best possible education through primary and secondary schools in my hometown of Mỹ Tho then the prestigious Lycée Yersin in Dalat. Again, by "fate and destiny" and with the help of USIS, I had my own two wings for my "Flight of the Eagle" from the Mekong Delta to Massachusetts, USA. I did not have to pinch myself but it seemed somewhat "unreal" even in the wildest dream of any Vietnamese youngster in the 1950s! Therefore, the graduation day at MIT was the last day of my long academic journey in both time and space. Before joining the rough, tough and mean world of business in New York City, I wanted to have a total view of my uphill and challenging road to the summit of the mountain.

It was through lots of sweat and tears but the results were more than good. Besides my continued and painful efforts there were many unpredictable elements as well which could only come by fate and destiny. I always started as a handicapped runner in the old five stages of this marathon: primary, junior high, high school, college and university stages. I began my first year of schooling in the very small village of Rạch Miễu, on the opposite side of the Mekong River by the Mỹ Tho ferry boat. The school was a little thatch roof wooden shelter built on compacted soil. My parents realized that I had no future in that miserable place and transferred me to the Mỹ Tho public primary school. I finished this first stage, lost *incognito* among the crowd. Then, I had to take a competitive entrance exam to Mỹ Tho junior high. It was a first scary challenge because if I could not make it, there was no acceptable private school in my hometown. Somehow my parents convinced me that a good education was indispensable and important for my future. In Vietnamese society, the scholar is ranked the highest class, next comes the farmer, then the artisan and last the merchant.

Many of my close friends and relatives would like to know about the academic life of twins because they know I have a twin brother. Very quickly, in a nutshell, I can say that both of us started with the same French Empire colonial school system. Like many kids, we did all sorts of pranks and we often got into fights with other boys. Whenever there was a fight at school, both of us automatically beat the other common enemy. It happened that we came out victorious every time and that was enough to stop future provocation or fighting. It was at Mỹ Tho junior high school that I became more conscious about achieving academic success. And it was about academic performance that made me believe there was something mean or ignorant about people when they think about child psychology in those days. Because we were twins, people often asked: "How come you are both from the same gene and the other half was better?" This made me feel even more conscious and aware of emulation and/or competition.

My twin Quí on the left and me in front of MIT chapel June, 1956

With my savings, I bought my twin a ticket with Holland America Line to visit MIT.

Sitting there in my room after the MIT graduation ceremony and ruminating about the ups and downs of my academic life, I had to admit it was sheer fate and destiny that I was able to pass the French Baccalaureate with the rare "*mention bien*" at the time which turned out to be the key to my "Black Box" for my "Flight of the Eagle" to America. It was something unbelievable but true for the little guy from the Mekong Delta to obtain his Master's degree in Mechanical Engineering at the prestigious MIT. It must be some sort of a miracle but not without sweat and tears!

I remembered well the French system for the Baccalaureate. I finished my French baccalaureate in Dalat with *"mention bien"*, the only one in six years at Yersin. I was valedictorian and earned The Grand Honor Prize from the King of Cambodia, His Majesty Norodom Sihanouk. In addition to the Prize of Sciences from the Mayor of Dalat, I concurrently was awarded the Prize of Valedictorian from the Association of Parents of Lycée Chasseloup-Laubat, Lycée Marie Curie and Lycée Yersin. All these academic results led me to the US State Department Fulbright scholarship to study engineering in America. That was how MIT became my destination.

Even now, thinking back about these student days, I must say that the few years at the Dalat Lycée Yersin did give me a tremendous fighting spirit to excel in my studies. Here, thanks must also be given to my twin who infused in me the sense of competition and determination to overcome whatever challenges and obstacles I had to confront. I said to myself then that whatever my twin could do I could do as well or even better.

The French educational system rates high school grades from zero to 20 on the final exams. A mark of 10 out of 20 will earn a "mention passable" meaning you pass.

In junior and senior high schools three levels of honors are given:

- A mark between 12 and 13.99 will earn a *"mention assez bien"* meaning you pass with *honors*
- A mark between 14 and 15.99 will earn a *"mention bien"* meaning you pass with *high honors*
- A mark of 16 or higher will earn a *"mention très bien"* meaning you pass with *highest honors*

Throughout our lives my twin and I competed with one another, often rather heatedly. In fact, as youngsters, we actually fought physically quite often. Therefore, it was a great encouragement to me that in his junior high school, my twin earned a "mention passable" while I was valedictorian with a "mention bien." My twin did not pass the French baccalaureate in Dalat. He was then sent to Paris to finish his high school. He eventually obtained a pharmacy degree and his doctorate. Then he worked for the CNRS (Centre de Recherche Scientifique) as Director of Research. This was no small achievement for one who had failed at his French high school in Dalat!

I was also a bit jealous that my twin was able to enjoy a much better material life in Paris with a rather wealthy uncle, while the uncle who took care of me was not at all able financially to send me to study in France and much less in the United States of America. As is commonly said, some are born with a silver spoon in their mouths and some are not. I did not get the silver spoon! And lacking the spoon, one has to pick up the shovel and dig hard. I did just that! Thanks again to my twin, I acquired at a very early age a competitive and fighting spirit in life. I often have the impression that my twin, having become a Parisian in the past 60 years, may continue to look down on me to some degree, perhaps because in his mind I was not able to receive a French education and lack the "sophistication" of a *Parisien*. I am quite happy with my life in San Francisco Bay over the past 40 years and never had the desire to move to anywhere else. I am certain my twin must think that his Parisian life is the very best in the world since Paris is a wonderful city with beautiful monuments.

Back to my room at MIT, I then tried to have some sleep and be ready for my trip to New York City, the Big Apple, for my new job.

The twin at Paris airport in 1976

CHAPTER 8

Work and Fun in New York City

The "Eagle Has Landed" on the Big Apple!

EVOLUTION OF THE NEW YORK SKYLINE

The "Eagle has landed" not on the moon but in New York City after five years of an adventuresome flight. Now "EAST meets WEST" but in the very heart of the New World. What a big breakthrough in my life. From my high school days in colonial Vietnam, I did hope that someday I could become an engineer and begin working in the United States to get sound professional skills and experiences before returning home to serve my country. Had that day really arrived when I was going to take that job in the extraordinary urban center called New York City?

New York City with Central Park

Lower Manhattan with ferries to Staten Island, Ellis Island and Statue of Liberty

Taking my maiden flight across the vast Pacific Ocean in 1952, little did I know that, of all the places, I would make a landing in 1957 in one of the largest and noisiest cities on earth: New York. Wow! What a total contrast in lifestyle from my five years in Pennsylvania and Massachusetts. Even further back to the beautiful, quiet campus of Lycée Yersin in Dalat, then the peaceful Lafayette College town of Easton and the busy high-tech Cambridge center of MIT, the sight of giant skyscrapers and the endless flows of people and cars in the Big Apple provoked a drastic change in the living environment. I already had something of a prejudice against New York City, though often considered a hard and mean place, it was at the same time the home of the United Nations Headquarters and the financial hub of Wall Street, and thus an important center for international diplomacy and business.

How Did I Get my First Job in New York City?

Two months before my graduation from MIT in June 1957, I got a letter from EBASCO (Electric Bond And Share Company) inviting me to New York City for an interview. EBASCO was a well-known engineering company designing and building electric power plants around the world. The job market for engineers in the 1950's was very attractive, especially after the Soviet Union launched the world first satellite, Sputnik.

I was very concerned about how to make a good first impression on the day of my interview. How should I meet the challenge of the interviewer? After seriously reviewing the fundamentals of power plant engineering and packing a sharp blue business suit with a white shirt, nice silk tie and well-polished shoes, I took the train from Boston to Penn Station, New York. The hotel reserved for me was on Broadway not far from the head office of EBASCO. To my surprise, during the interview, I was not asked about my engineering knowledge, my general qualification for the job. On the contrary, my future boss Mr. Metzger, explained to me how I could advance fast in this company and my job would be secured. The company's future work load was solid for years to come due to increasing demand for electric energy around the world. Later I learned that Mr. Metzger was an MIT alumnus. Obviously, he relied on my tough training at MIT and did not need to check on my engineering background. Well, that was a lucky first break in my career.

Now my down to earth problem was where to stay in this new place?

Manhattan

Aerial view of New York City

Aerial view of New York City

Getting settled down for the first time in the Big Apple was not an easy task. I came up with a short check list for finding my new home:

1. Easy access to my office near City Hall and Broadway.
2. Safe area.
3. Short distance from Columbia University for my night school.
4. Close to subway for convenient daily commute.
5. Last but not least, availability of good "Chop stick culture" food

Eureka! I found a studio on Cathedral Parkway, 110th Street near Broadway, a place owned by a Jewish lady, a refugee from Nazi Germany during WWII. I had tried a nearby good New Asia restaurant as well. The rent was $100 a month; my salary $600 a month. No big deal! It was just a modest, functional and convenient place for a quick start. Comparing this to a campus room, I felt dangerously isolated in case of emergency. Alone in a room in a skyscraper among thousands of skyscrapers was not my life style. I felt like living in a pigeon hole with a sense of claustrophobia. From the window of my studio apartment, I saw another window of another high wall. It was not any better than some modern prison cells seen on TV. Was this how millions of New Yorkers live? What a big shock and surprise for my preconceived opinion of life in a highly developed country.

I did not like this new style of social environment: too impersonal, a lack of human touch. During my last five years, everyday and everywhere I met my roommates, my classmates, my schoolmates, my professors, my dishwasher mates, my fellow waiters and even the cook of Watson hall in his living quarters. Here in New York, every day and everywhere I met but strangers! As a matter of fact I remembered clearly the time I had the flu in my studio apartment on the 10th floor of the building. What a miserable, feeling of insecurity! I could be dead for a week before people would discover my corpse!

I began looking for friends living in New York and getting in touch with new acquaintances to feel less lonely. During my four years at Lafayette, Pennsylvania, only 70 miles away from New York, I had two Vietnamese friends working for the Voice of America (VOA) in that city: Chấn and Quan. Recently, there was a new one Bùi kiến Thành, my 1944 math classmate in Saigon. Now Thành had obtained a very important job responsible for investing in Wall Street the foreign exchange funds of the Vietnamese government. His nice office was at a walking distance from mine. At noon, we often went to Chinatown's Mott Street for Dim Sum. He had from time to time visitors from Vietnam and invited me to his home for dinner. One of those visitors was the well-known Mr. Huỳnh văn Lang, the head of Vietnam foreign exchange office. I learned later that Lang was the right-hand man of the powerful Cần Lao party chief Mr. Ngô đình Nhu, brother of President Ngô đình Diệm. For social contacts, the very popular and best place in town was the International House known as I-House.

For the time being, I had to hurry up to get ready to go to work as soon as possible. On work days, I took the nearby subway at Cathedral Parkway and Broadway then got off at the downtown Chambers Street station, a short walk to the office. It was a very rapid but noisy transit. During rush hour all trains were fully packed and you could tell the typical New Yorkers by their special way of reading the New York Times folded in half in a very crowded place! For moving around town, it was a necessity to know well the subway and bus maps of Manhattan. One night after work, on the subway home, I got out at 125th street to go to Columbia night school. By mistake I walked into 125th but on the Harlem side. It was an all-black area, a really scary place for me especially at night! I hurried back into the subway and got out at the other side of 125th street. That was what I mean by the mix of the awful with the beautiful, the dangerous with the secured area. From that day, I made sure to memorize the detailed maps of both of these systems of transportation and to learn how to use them the right way. Owning a car for use in town was unthinkable for me because of difficult parking and heavy traffic.

While studying at Lafayette College, I loved to visit New York with its famous landmarks. But now I should live here and it was a very different and difficult situation. I guessed New York might be like Paris, a place for a pleasant visit but not for a permanent stay.

The best job of my life. Why?

Transportation Building on Broadway: my office on the 17th floor

The technology side of the projects assigned to me was not of the state of the art research and development type. It was down to earth design engineering, procurement of equipment, construction (EPC) and delivery of power plants on a turn-key basis. EBASCO had done this type of work for so many years around the world. I remembered seeing in the office that the Tokyo Electric Plant No.1 was done by EBASCO and the Japanese then copied it and built their No. 2, 3 and 4! I took advantage of the company's existing engineering design and specifications and adapted them to my projects at the new sites. I did work on two 10,000 KW plants, one for Guayaquil, Ecuador, the other for Matanzas, Cuba. In 1957, Castro was still in the underground.

As a compensation for the hardship in the Big Apple, I felt a great sense of relief and good fortune to have obtained the best job of my life. In retrospect, after forty years of professional activities and hard work, I could say that by luck, fate and destiny my first job in New York City was the most enjoyable. How often could I say: "It was fun to go to work?" Why? I discerned two most important factors: the interesting engineering learning curve for my career and the warm human relations of the team. Of course, high salary was important too but at the start I was willing to make sacrifice as long as I could learn a lot from the job. I found all those conditions at EBASCO. My boss Mr. Mortimer Metzger, in his 50's, was a friendly, competent engineer from my own MIT School. He supervised my project manager Jack Rubinstein, also in his 50's, a very jovial and open-minded friend. I was Jack's assistant. The rest of the team were two draftsmen Mario Vitelly, an Italian American, George Sikorsky, a Russian immigrant during WWII, and our young secretary Olga Berkov, another immigrant from Ukraine. This was one of the best teams in my career. There was neither conflict of interest nor personality incompatibility among team members. We really worked hard in harmony and high spirit. What a break to be able to enjoy life at the work place! Jack and I had also a very unique work relationship. I volunteered to do all the tedious calculations for the project because I was looking for solid experience. Jack loved to relax, check my work and we co-signed the results. We both were happy in our personal own ways. At lunch time, in appreciation of my hard work, Jack volunteered to tell me a lot of good jokes including the salty ones. After so many years of sweat in the office designing nothing but power plants, Jack wanted to take it a little easy at his cruising speed. What was routine for Jack was really new to me. It was a wonderful trade-off. I loved my calculations of steam balances and a lot of other items like pumps, piping, controls, heat exchangers, cooling towers etc… in a power plant project and Jack loved to check and approve my calculations. On weekends, he knew I was alone and did not hesitate to invite me to his home in New Jersey. We went together to his Unitarian church and lunched at his home with the family. I was lucky to have "a friend in need is a friend indeed." I would admit that the very enjoyable and interesting job at EBASCO reduced a lot of my initial reluctance to live in a city like New York.

What did I learned in this international corporation?

I learned that in the 50's American international corporations dominated the field of electric energy in Central and South America. The firm EBASCO signed a contract with American and Foreign Power Company for the engineering design, procurement, construction and finally turn-key delivery to its client. In turn for the complete integration in this industry, American and Foreign Power operated the plant and sold electric energy to its local consumers. That was total integration and monopoly.

It was a wonderful place to acquire the needed project experience, including composition of the working team and organization chart of the whole company. It was instructive, valuable experience and fun too. It all made me remember the French saying "Aimer ce qu'on fait et bien faire ce qu'on aime" i.e. "Love what we do and do well what we love." On the business side, I learned that good public relations with companies supplying equipment for the project were very necessary in a competitive market. For instance, during our design phase, sales engineers visited us in our office and explained to us the state of the art of their products, their high efficiency equipment. At noon break, a part of their function was to invite us to a business lunch in downtown Manhattan. What a delightful job. I had a really unusual break with Jack, my senior partner. Looking back at my entire professional career of over four decades, I could say that my job in New York was the one which gave me the most satisfaction and fun. No rivalry, no jealous attitude, no ill will, and nothing like that during my 17 years of public service in Vietnam. In Vietnam with each change of government there was an opportunity for politicians to replace the CEOs of state-run enterprises for the interests of their political parties. Talking about working relationships, I must say that one of my most striking records in Saigon was to be able to keep the same top position continuously during 12 years of the industrial development of South Vietnam at a time of political unrest and raging war. How was I able to keep my interesting job that long? I will go into details in chapter 13 about my work in Saigon.

To avoid loneliness at age 26 in the Big Apple, humanely and naturally with Eve and the Serpent roaming around, I would have to look for a companion in life and start a family. At this stage I had enough income and a stable job from a well-established international company. That was probably the reason why suddenly two important and complex challenges crossed my mind: sex and marriage. What a huge and complicated milestone of life. I just went through five years of academic stress for good grades but, in school, the nature of the problem seemed clear and neat. This challenge of sex and marriage started a new learning curve for me. How to choose a compatible wife in New York City? I could not even find and meet any Vietnamese girl in the Big Apple! Then should I think of inter-racial marriage? It sounded like walking either on thin ice or into a mysterious and explosive minefield. I scratched my head a lot and remembered two precedent inter-racial marriages in my extended family. These two cases might teach me a lesson.

In 1945, my cousin NTD from Vietnam continued his dentistry study in Paris after his Hanoi University was shut down by the war. He needed English to keep up to date with American dental journal publications. His teacher happened to be an American lady from Chicago. They ended up as a happily married couple for more than 50 years. They settled down in Revin, Ardennes, France with four successful children. The whole family integrated fully into French society. I would say it was a real successful case of inter-racial union with a happy ending. Another cousin KHH left Vietnam for Bordeaux, France in the early 40's. After finishing his medical school, he opened a medical lab in Villeneuve-sur-Lot and became the richest man in town. He married a French lady and had two children. They ended up in divorce. It was a real unhappy situation. The problem was personality conflict rather than racial. In both situations, they all lived in France, a more liberal and open society. If they were living in Vietnam, a generally conservative Confucian society, they certainly would face additional difficulties. All of this review taught me a lesson: Vietnam and specifically my traditional family were not ready for my inter-racial marriage. It could be a disaster for many reasons: Open hostility and intimidation, negative stereotyping, derogatory comments, stares, insults, jibes, slights, whispers and a sense of isolation, and family rejection.

Alone in New York City, I had to do very serious and difficult soul searching on this tricky matter. To me, marriage was already quite a challenge in life, surely the biggest, whether inter-racial or not, but it would be more advisable to avoid additional problems whenever possible! Besides the conventional problems caused by society, there were always interracial marriage personal challenges between the partners. According to a Vietnamese saying" To measure the rivers and the oceans is easy, but there is no yardstick to measure the human mind and soul." It could be very romantic and exciting to love someone different but the attraction could not always overcome everything that life might throw at the couple. For instance, the inter-racial marriage may have to face cultural differences regarding matters such as religion, diet, birth control, parenting preferences, grief, finances, sex, extended family relationships, gender roles, communication styles, customs and traditions. What could cause an inter-racial marriage to fall apart would be the inability of a couple to handle their differences and also their failure to resolve stress and prejudice created by others. The bottom line for me was: no marriage as long as I lived in New York. The last dangerous warning for me was a French saying: "Le coeur a ses raisons que la raison ne connait point." i.e. "The Heart has its reasons which reason knows not."
But caution: a crush was still a crush or "coup de foudre!" meaning "struck by lightning" as the French would say. "Love at first sight!" in English may sound more romantic but I had to be very prudent and careful to avoid walking into that minefield.

Fun in New York City

One of the best places in New York for social activities and contacts with new friends was the International House. This well-known I-House was a private, non-profit residence and program center for graduate students, scholars engaging in research, trainees and interns. I-House's 700 resident members attended various universities and schools throughout the City of New York, including Columbia University, Juilliard School, Actors' Studio Drama School, New York University, the Manhattan School of Music, the Union Theological Seminary in the City of New York, the Teachers College, and the City University of New York, among others. Students came from over 100 countries with about one-third of those coming from the United States. The past Honorary Chairman of the Board was Dwight Eisenhower.

Entrance to the International House

New York was also known for its world-famous entertainment programs. Every year countries around the world brought to New York their best cultural shows. With my limited time available for fun, I succeeded to enjoy some of the best programs in the world. The following photos illustrate the many places I had the chance to visit: Christmas show at Radio City Music Hall, Moscow's Moiseyev high flying dancers, London Royal Ballet, Tokyo Taiko Drum Music, Yugoslavian folk dances, Tristan and Isolde at the Metropolitan Opera House. For classical music, I had a chance to listen to the New York Philharmonic with André Kostalanetz.

My first contact with New York City was very negative. I found that it was not a very neat city. The landscape and architecture were pell-mell, mixed up, very heterogeneous. The ugly mixed too often with the beautiful and sophisticated. In the Saigon USIS library, I had learned that New York was the most populous city in the United States. It exerted a significant impact on the world in areas of commerce, finance, media, art, fashion, research, technology, education, and entertainment. The reality was rather deceptive. It gave me the impression of a "dog eat dog" place.

While studying at Lafayette College, Easton, Pa 65 miles away, I loved to visit New York with its famous landmarks. But now I should live here and it was a very different and difficult situation. I missed the green, open space i.e. nature. That was my surrounding since childhood in the Mekong delta, to the highlands of Dalat. Even in the United States, the last five years, I lived on the ground floor surrounded by green trees and green grass of the campus. Now skyscrapers surrounded and dominated me everywhere. Air and noise pollution made it even worse. There were no tree lined streets and green lawn. Always concrete, asphalt, stone, bricks all over town. I felt choked.

For me, New York was like Paris, a place for a pleasant visit but not for a permanent stay.

Times Square, a major cultural venue in the city

Manhattan city at night

My initial impression of New York might have been distorted because the city was so huge that if I happened to know only the tail part of the elephant, I missed the ivory front part. Now that my job and my career learning curve were under control, I went to Columbia campus to register for the MBA, 3 nights a week, a very useful tool for a future Engineering Executive.

Columbia University, my night school three times a week

Why fun in New York City?

Some fun at this stage was important because before NYC, I was under constant pressure to get good grades in order to graduate and obtain a scholarship. The fear of failure was so great that all sacrifices seemed natural. Time for study always got first priority. Time for fun was always last priority.

Second, any time available after study was devoted to earning money for self-support. Now for the first time in my life I had a regular, comfortable salary. So, for the first time in five years I could afford to pay for entertainment and gourmet food.

Third, the job was stable and working conditions very relaxed. I was lucky to belong to a very good team that worked together in perfect harmony. No work headache.

The view from the top of the Empire State building was a must. Central Park was behind these skyscrapers. Visitors to New York went to the top of the Empire State building like in Paris people wanted to be on the top of the Eiffel Tower

Empire State building, Tallest in the world from 1931 to 1972

US OPEN at Forest Hills, Long Island, N.Y.

I had the unique chance of watching the famous 1958 US OPEN at Forest Hills with Poncho Gonzales vs. Ken Rosewall

I took the Ferry at Battery Park to visit the Statue of Liberty

On weekends, I liked to take a walk in Central Park first for exercise but mostly for observing how New Yorkers lived in their hometown with their various social activities. Lunch at the boathouse was a good choice for that objective.

Central Park restaurant

Every year, countries from all over the world brought to New York City some of their best shows. For instance, I had the chance to watch in 1957 the Moiseyev dance company from Moscow. There was another good one from Yugoslavia.

Four seasons in Central Park

Central Park was the place for the outdoor and good food any season of the year.

Annual Figure Skating Championships, Wollman Rink Central Park

During Christmas time, Rockefeller Center was a very popular place. There may be no holiday highlight quite like The Rockefeller Center Christmas Tree. Giant in stature and sentiment, the Tree has a true crowd-delighter for over 75 years.

Christmas at Rockefeller Center

Radio City Music Hall

Radio City Music Hall Rockettes

Radio City Music Hall: Moscow high flying Moiseyev Dance Company

New York Natural History Museum

Guggenheim Museum

Guggenheim Museum, a new architectural concept

Chinatown Manhattan is where we could get the same kind of foods as in mainland China if we knew how to order them

Gastronomy in New York

In those days there was no Internet and Google to look for good food in the BIG APPLE. However, I could rely on the yellow pages and find all the gourmet places that this City offered from no star to three stars and for hundreds of diversified international cuisines. I remember best the classic American Steak House, not very often found around the world in the 50's. That was the Red Coach on chic Fifth Avenue. The Maître d' rolled a silver top cart to the red leather dining room. Near your table, he carved a nice pink slice of Prime Ribs au jus to fill your warm plate to the border. An oven baked, buttered potato and a side dish of blue cheese salad completed the meal followed by cheese cake for dessert. The next day might be another Japanese Sashimi dinner or a Korean BBQ short rib special…

In 1957, I was very curious about this Automat restaurant where you cou

ld not see waiters or cooks!

Again it was fate and destiny

EBASCO sent me to an international conference in NYC on the topic: *Demand of Electric Energy around the World* at the Waldorf Astoria. By coincidence, I happened to sit next to Mr. George P. Case, General Manager of Esso, Saigon, Vietnam. He was back to the U.S. for a vacation at his home in White Plains, NY. I told him that I was from Saigon and I had not seen my country for seven years because of my study and work in the U.S. Talking about Saigon really made me feel homesick. Mr. Case was kind enough to invite me to his home so we had a chance to talk about what Vietnam was like since I left. He seemed very sincere, open and wholehearted. He did give me a round trip train ticket and offered to pick me up at the White Plains commuter station. Mrs. Case prepared a delicious rice curry lunch for the occasion. Mr. Case had been General Manager in India before coming to Viet Nam. I began to feel homesick again wishing to see my dear parents the soonest possible. The Asian meal of rice curry triggered my homesickness again. After Mr. Case's meeting and talk about Viet Nam, he offered me a seemingly executive position as an assistant Operations Manager at his Saigon office. The job paid much better than a high-ranking government job at the department director level in a ministry. I accepted to return and work in Vietnam. He and Mrs. Case suggested to me a shopping list of good but rare clothing for Saigon weather. He warned me that after entering Saigon, it would be almost impossible to obtain an exit visa. The reason being the government policy of keeping young males in the country because of the mobilization law. That meant: see the world as much as possible and not expect any future travel to foreign countries once back in Vietnam. Accordingly, I did a lot of homework to maximize my precious opportunity to see the world in view of my return to Vietnam.

It took me only one day to make up my mind and decide to terminate my good job at EBASCO immediately after I was able to finalize my plan of 90 days around the world by Pan American Airways. A new milestone had been cast.

PART IV

Time to Go Home

CHAPTER 9

New York – Saigon in 90 days
Via Pan Am

1958

Touring Western Europe 15,000 Km
then
Flying Home from Paris to Saigon 15,000 Km

NY Times Square

Saigon Central Market

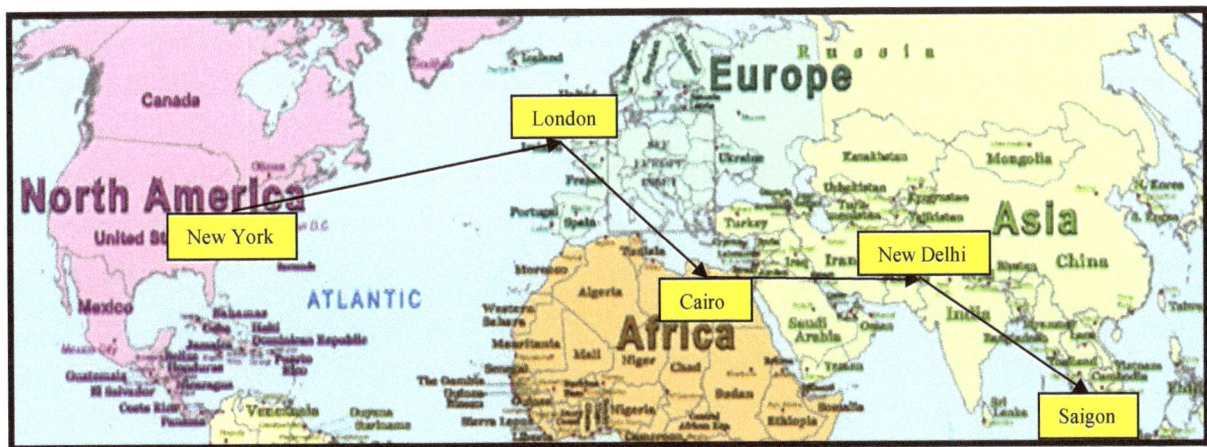

New York - Saigon in 90 Days, 1958

Again it was fate and destiny. Right after MIT, I had my ideal job in 1957 with Ebasco, (Electric Bonds and Shares Corporation) in New York City. One day in 1958, the corporation sent me to an international conference on the World Demand of Energy at the luxurious Waldorf-Astoria hotel in Midtown Manhattan. By pure coincidence I sat next to a participant with a tag G. P. Case, Esso Saigon, on his vest. He happened to be the General Manager of Esso Vietnam taking vacations at his home in White Plains, NY. I was warmly invited for lunch at his family place. He offered me a round trip train ticket and picked me up at White Plains station. Briefly, after a historic *rice* lunch with excellent spicy Indian curry cooked by his wife, he made me feel very homesick. By the way, he had been Esso general manager in India and knew a lot about hot and delicious curry.

In retrospect, he succeeded in convincing me to be happy in my "chopstick culture" with my parents in Saigon no matter what. Then he offered me a job as Assistant Operations Manager in his Saigon office. After seven years away from my parents and extended family, I felt very eager to hear all his good stories about life in Saigon. Mr. Case had plenty of experiences to lure me home. I made up my mind quite easily to leave New York to be close to my parents. The preparation for this special long trip began. He also warned me that because of the possible government mobilization law for the war effort, it would be difficult for me to obtain an exit visa, once I had returned to Vietnam. Naturally, I made sure to visit and learn as much as possible about the outside free world before going back to my native land. He suggested a list of goods to buy knowing well what were hard to find and expensive in Saigon. I remembered I bought a lot of typical New York light Dacron-cotton non-iron shirts, cotton blankets, sheets and towels.

Normally people worked all their life to save some money and before or during retirement would make trips or take cruises around the world to enjoy life. For me at 27, with the money I had saved in New York, I would like to see the world as much and as soon as possible at my early age. Why? In this way I could collect the best things around the world and used them the rest of my life. Furthermore, youth would give me the health and strength required for real adventurous travel activities.

I decided to visit as many countries as feasible on the way back to Saigon by Pan American World Airways, the largest international air carrier in 1958. With the help of my good friend Lou Lou from Pan Am, New York 5th Avenue office, I planned to take-off from Idlewild Airport with stops over in Lisbon, Madrid, Nice, London, Paris, Milan, Athens, Cairo, Teheran, Bombay, New Deli, Calcutta, Rangoon, Bangkok, Phnom Penh and finally Saigon. In 1952, I came to the US by plane via Manila, Guam, Midway, Wake, Honolulu, San Francisco, Pittsburgh, Harrisburg and Easton Pennsylvania. In 1956, I continued to Boston then New York in 1957. At 27, I felt very fortunate to be able to make a trip around the world with an extra 15,000 km motoring in Western Europe. Eastern Europe was off limit because of the cold war Iron Curtain.

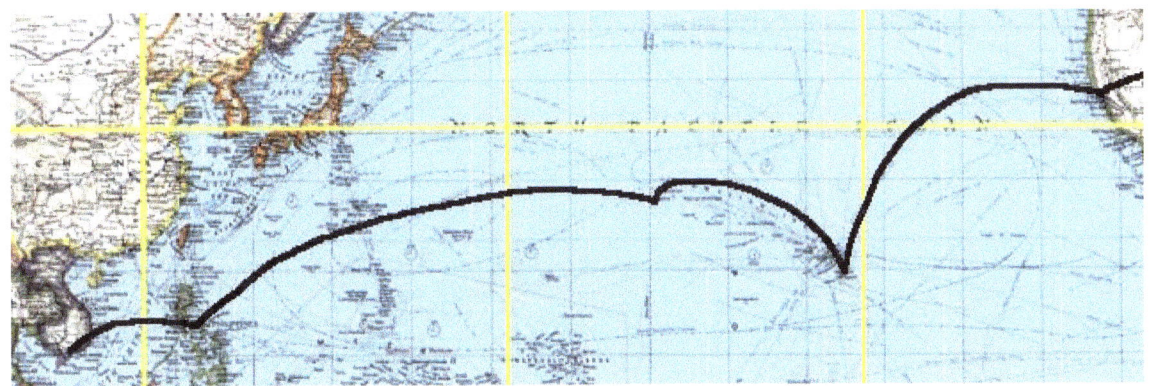

1952 trip: Saigon-Manila-Guam-Wake-Midway-Honolulu-San Francisco by DC-B

From New York to Lisbon, Madrid, Nice, London I was traveling alone. However, when touring Western Europe by camping and B&B, I had the company of my twin Khương Hữu Quí from Paris and my brother Khương Hữu Cân from Saigon joining me for more fun. On my way to Europe I had to stop in Nice to see my sister Chị Ba and my brother-in-law Nguyễn Văn Khuê who retired there since 1950.

Michelin Travel Guides & Pan Am World guide

I used the above tools for planning my long voyage home.

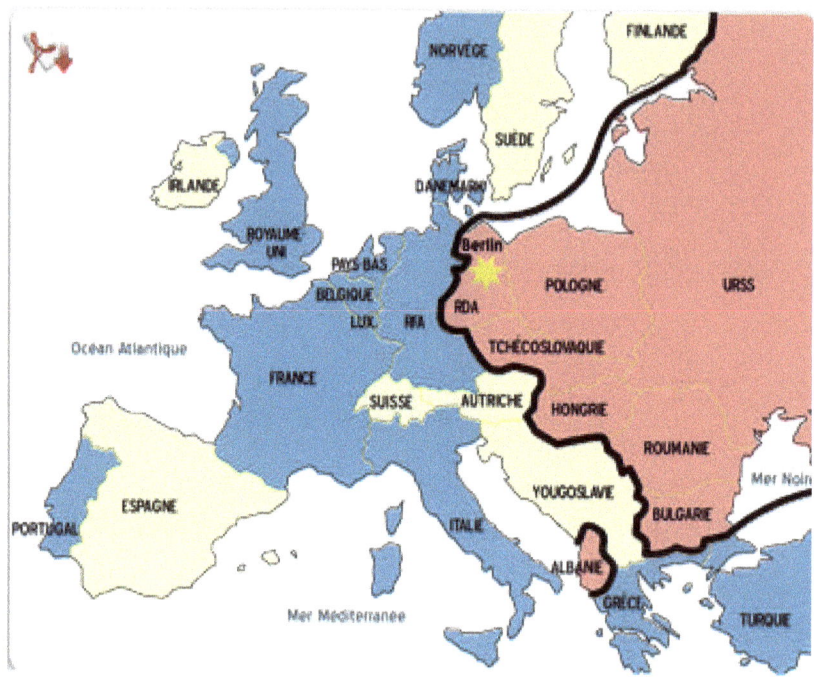

Map of Europe with Iron Curtain

I had fixed a rendezvous with my two brothers at the Brussels World's Fair at Noon June 15, 1958 under the famous Atomium. (See photo of the iconic structure.) We wanted to see together the famous Brussels EXPO 58. There was something very exciting about this fair because on October 4, 1957 the Russian launched the world first artificial Earth satellite. This triggered the Space Race, a part of the larger Cold War. The whole world was watching the competition between the Soviet Union and the USA at the WORLD'S FAIR 58.

Brussel's World's Fair 58 & the Atomium

In the 50's Pan Am published The Encyclopedia of Travel, 1,014 pages thick known as the "bible" for tourists. I depended entirely on the New York Pan Am agent for planning my ticket and booking all the hotel reservations for my trip home because of my ignorance of the wide world.

My two brothers would arrive from Paris with a four door French Renault Dauphine; I flew in from London with my camping gear, a Bell Howell 16mm, 3 lenses movie camera and an American Express Travelers check book of a few thousand dollars. That was how our European camping tour was planned.

I took off from New York in June 1958, missing the opening of Pan Am jet age by a few months. The airline inaugurated its world's first nonstop transatlantic jet service from Idlewild to Paris Le Bourget on October 26, 1958, with a Boeing 707 Clipper America. 1958 was the beginning of the Golden Age for Commercial Flight: "White Gloves" quality service and very comfortable amenities for the passengers. The piston-driven planes of those days were the Lockheed Constellation and Douglas DC-7. For shorter distances, the Turboprop (turbine-driven propellers) Viscounts were popular. All those planes couldn't fly above bad weather the way jet-powered airplanes could do.

In 1958 the high cost of a world ticket was affordable for only an elite few. Seats had generous legroom, three to six inches more than today in coach. Travelers enjoyed lots of empty seats to spread out into as well. The load factor, or percentage of seats filled, was quite low. Airlines competed on the basis of service and not on the basis of price. It was the "tourists market". Most of the passengers seemed to represent well to do middle class. They were in general nicely dressed. Meals in flight were like gourmet foods with sleek design glass, porcelain dishes and silverware on table cloth. No plastics or paper plates! In fact the artistic design of the different airlines' was so beautiful that passengers wished to buy them as collectables.

Best of PAN AM in 1958: DC-7

In June 1958, my flight started from NY City with refueling stops in Gander (Newfoundland,) Santa Maria (Azores Islands) then Lisbon. The greatest pleasant difference in air travel those days was the total absence of problems and headaches at the airport created by today's terrorists!

LISBON

My very first landing in the Old World was Lisbon. While studying in the US, many of my schoolmates often talked about their "Old Countries" because most of their families were immigrants from Europe. They gave me a general knowledge of their native lands. Now I had the opportunity to observe firsthand the real Old World. My first impression was the abundance of beautiful, imposing, majestic old castles and monuments all over the place. There was a big difference in the young country like the USA. No ancient castles, only a few imported ones and reassembled like California's Hearst Castle!

My first shock was the old world eating habits. In the States, I used to eat dinner around 6 PM. Here lunch, often lasting over an hour, was served between 1 and 3 o'clock, and dinner generally began only after 8 or 9 o'clock. And people really took time to enjoy their meals. Portugal's traditional cooking has Mediterranean influence: gazpacho was a popular soup of tomatoes, cucumber, onions, garlic, chilies and vinegar. I tried the national dish, Bacalhau which was actually salted cod with nearly as many ways to cook salt cod as days of the year. In the old times, Portuguese were known for fishing cod in Newfoundland, Canada. I could not forget another local delicacy, the national chorizo sausage. Of course, one should drink the excellent local Porto and Madeira wines. At the fish market, I saw for the first time merchants carrying fish on their head in a metallic cylindrical pan. In 1958, fast food the way we knew it in the States, had not reached the shores of Europe or the world.

Walking downtown, I was impressed by the iconic buildings and monuments (See photos below) and the country's glorious past. I was surprised to learn that a small country like Portugal had a great Empire around the world: colonies in Africa, Brazil, Macau, Timor and enclaves in India.

60-year-old blue tile shop

Light rail downtown

Lighthouse Belem Tower

Tram

Monument to the Discoveries

Ajuda National Palace

The Palace of Queluz.

Old Lisbon narrow street

Estoril, 15 km from Lisbon, had a pleasant beach front promenade and the playground of the rich and famous with the greatest casino of Europe. My next flight took me to Madrid.

MADRID

The Red and Yellow national colors of Spain around town reminded me of similar colors at home during our TET celebration in Annam, Central Vietnam.

Annam flag *Spain flag*

This city had some similarities with Lisbon: great monuments, palaces, and late eating hours with special exciting flamboyant flamenco dance.

Museo del Prado *Plaza Mayor built by Philip III (1598–1621)*

World famous Serrano ham

Royal Palace, city central plaza, 1764   *Flamenco dance*

City Hall

I shall never forget the seafood stalls which sell paella, tapas and delicacies like urchins, oysters and razor clams.

NICE

After Madrid, I continued with PAN AM to Nice to see my sister Chị Ba who retired there in 1950. She was surprised that I stayed at the luxurious 3 star hotel Negresco downtown. Actually by ignorance, I let the airline do all the booking for me! This beautiful French seaside resort town of Nice impressed me with so many luxurious yachts of really wealthy people. The beach was however very rough with small gravel; no white sand like in Carmel, California. It's time for me to enjoy the Provence cuisine: Ratatouille, les Petits Farcis stuffed with minced veal and beef, bread crumbs, and vegetables, Salade Niçoise usually with anchovies, peppers, courgettes (zucchini) and their flowers, and onions.

Cote d'Azur Beach   *Negresco Hotel*

LONDON

Big Ben   *English breakfast*

I continued my trip to London. My first surprise was a huge English breakfast compared with the one in America. There's a ridiculous amount there! Bacon and eggs or a fry-up: bacon rashers, fried eggs, sausages, beans, hash browns, black pudding, fried tomato and mushrooms served with toast on the side, and orange juice. It was also common to see an assortment of condiments, including jams and ketchup, fresh fruit. Classically, a fry up is accompanied with numerous cups of strong black tea or coffee. A real calorie fest but delicious! On the other hand, I found fish and chips for lunch very reasonable, simple and tasty.

A typical London street with double deck bus, phone booth

Tower Bridge *Changing of the guard at Buckingham palace*

I remembered asking a policeman the best places to eat, and to my surprise all of them were not English. I guessed in 1958 London was still known for "English boiled dinner". In the 21th century however, many of the world best restaurants are in London!

BELGIUM

My two brothers and I met at the Brussels World's Fair at Noon June 15, 1958 at the very foot of the famous Atomium. I had not seen them for seven years. We had a great, joyful reunion celebration with fancy, tasty Belgian beers, pairing with national special foods.

World's Fair entrance

Varieties of coiled boudin (blood sausage), shrimps street food

Sole Meunière　　*Sweet-sour steak and ale stew*　　*Mussels with French fries*

Actually, Belgians invented *frites*, way back in 1781.

Brothers' reunion in Belgium, 1958
L to R: Me, Brother Khương Hữu Cân and my twin Khương Hữu Quí

The Russian Pavilion

The American Pavilion

Interior of the Russian pavilion. This could be identified as the start of the cold war between Russia and America, or at the least, the beginning of the space race with a Model of the Sputnik.

Brussels Flower Carpet summer 58 *Pissing boy*

Legend told of a boy awoken by a fire. He put out the fire with his urine saving the king's castle from burning down, 1618.

Brussels Culinary Evening walk *Belgian waffles*

Who wouldn't want to go to a place called the Beer Planet? I knew for the first time that in Belgium there were two rival ethnic groups speaking two different languages: Dutch-Flemish and French.

THE NETHERLANDS

Royal Palace, Amsterdam

Netherlands windmills and cheese

The big draws these days were the fantastically preserved 18th-century windmills. Now the UNESCO World Heritage Sites, the 19 Kinderdijk windmills, built between 1722 and 1761, are still the largest surviving concentration of windmills in the Netherlands.

It is true to say that every year hundreds of thousands of tourists flock to catch a glimpse of these spectacular quilted farmlands before the flowers are cut and sold to florists and supermarkets around the world.

With the impression of being in the Italian Venice, Amsterdam welcomed me with her wonderful canals. Best tourist attractions could be easily accessed by boat tour or water taxi - including most of the major museums and art galleries. It's fun to just simply stroll along the smaller, quieter streets that line the waterways. One such neighborhood was the Grachtengordel and its many small bridges and quaint 17th-century homes. Explore these 400-year-old streets with countless examples of beautiful architecture, small boutique shops, cafés, and hotels, as well as many quaint colorful gardens.

The Rijksmuseum, a Dutch Treasure Trove   The Garden of Europe

Exploring Amsterdam's Canals   Dikes

It must be remembered that much of the country is below sea level and therefore relies upon impressive dikes. You can see evidence of the engineering project known as the Delta Works. This awe-inspiring project has been declared one of the Seven Wonders of the Modern World.

Each day during our trip, we decided the choice of a scenic route, the best interest points, the specialty foods along the way, as well as alternating between camping, gasthaus, auberge, inn or B&B…

1958, Camping in Groningen, Netherlands

I brought my modern tent from New York, and my twin brought his Renault Dauphine from Paris for the tour. In the lowland zone, the campground was often fairly wet.

I learned that the popular Dutch herrings are traditionally eaten by holding the fish by the tail and dunking it into your mouth with your head thrown back. If that doesn't seem appealing, herring can also be eaten in bite size pieces or on a sandwich called *broodje haring*.

If you're in Amsterdam you would see that many locals use the bicycle as main means of transportation to get around town. The number of bicycles I saw on the streets of Amsterdam was incredible. There were more bicycles than cars; even more bicycles than people in this city. The big difference was that here in Amsterdam people did not have to use locks for their bicycles; it was not the case in most Asian and European countries.

To be honest: looking into someone else's living room and seeing how they live would be very interesting. And in Holland, I noticed that the curtains in the houses were usually wide open so that you wouldn't even need to do anything other than shamelessly cast a glance into the domestic idyll as you passed by.

Cheese farm

We indulged in cheese sampling at a dutch cheese farm. The staff, dressed in traditional costumes greeted us and uncovered all the cheese samples for us to try.

Red Light District. From brothels to sex shops, to museums, the Amsterdam RLD left nothing to the imagination. What I had heard about this place was true. Women, of all nationalities, paraded their wares in red-fringed window parlors. I saw busloads of Japanese tourists with their cameras. This was proof enough that the RLD deserved a visit, if not a little look in.

Red Light District (RLD)

DENMARK

Denmark known for its extensive and generous cradle-to-grave welfare

It took the top spot on the United Nation's World Happiness Report, 2013 & 2014 & 2016. What I saw then in 1958 is still true today. It's home to one of the world's oldest running monarchies.

The Amalienborg Castle   *Changing of the guard*

I visited the Amalienborg Castle, the main residence of the royal family. They have a changing of the guard at the main palace complex every day. However, there was no fence for the protection of the country's leader, a sign of a democratic, civilized society. The Little Mermaid based on the fairy tale of Hans Christian Andersen has become an icon and a symbol of Copenhagen. It remains the most revered symbol of Copenhagen and Denmark's most photographed statue.

Little Mermaid

Everywhere were displayed amazing examples of architecture and engineering. No wonder Denmark has been considered the home of the Lego building block.

The Nyhavn Canal

Egeskov Castle, 1554, a public park

Tivoli Gardens

World famous Tivoli Gardens was founded in 1843 and became a national treasure and an international attraction and amusement park in Copenhagen. It is probably the best in Europe but I found it not a match to Disneyland and the Orlando Theme Park.

Tivoli Gardens

Tivoli Gardens is also the preferred spot for the locals to go and spend the day.

Tivoli Gardens at night *City Hall*

I learned that the Danes value their privacy highly, especially in the large city of Copenhagen. I have come to think that the Danes don't lose their cool. If they get upset, they will tell the person off in a cool and collected way. Don't be surprised by frank opinions. Danes don't sugar-coat to win your favor. They believe an honest approach is the best one. If you ask a question, expect an honest answer. The art of *Danish hygge* (coziness) means creating a nice, warm atmosphere and enjoying the good things in life with good people around you. It's the eating and drinking – preferably sitting around the table for hours on end discussing the big and small things in life.

I tasted the following local dishes: gravlax, a common Scandinavian dish made from raw salmon which is cured with salt, dill and sugar; meatballs with pickled cabbage, potatoes and beetroot; Danish pancake balls; and Nordic ligonberries and cloudberries.

NORWAY

From Denmark we took our car via the Frederikshavn ferry to Oslo.

Oslo's City Hall and Waterfront

I tried a typical Norwegian meal: The top food was Grilled Salmon - fishing being such a huge industry in Norway. The English translation for the dish called "stick meat" is made from salted and dried lamb's ribs steamed over birch sticks. Norwegian sausage is served in a thin tortilla made from potatoes and flour.

I ate blue whale steak. It was completely different from fish and the texture is exactly like beefsteak! Whale hunting has a long tradition in the Scandinavian region, so if you don't fully understand the reasons and history behind why they do something, don't criticize local practices.

Royal residence

Nobel peace center

In Norway, we made a scenic round trip Oslo-Bergen. This was a super natural highway following miles of mountain streams to the Atlantic Ocean passing by many fjords and wooden stave churches of medieval Christian denomination.

The scenic route following pure mountain stream

Fjord Trolltunga 190 km from Bergen *Restored 13th century Heddal stave church*

Borgund Stavkirke stave church *Tørrfisk, unsalted and cold air-dried fish*

Borgund Stavkirke is the only stave church at Laerdal to have remained unchanged since the Middle Ages and built entirely of wood, 1150.

A notable Norwegian fish dish is *Tørrfisk*, unsalted and cold air-dried fish (cod, haddock or Pollack,) a tradition since the 12th century. Norway's national drink *is akevitt* 'water of life', popular throughout Scandinavia.

Bergen has become a symbol of Norway's cultural heritage and has gained a place on UNESCO's World Heritage List.

Fish Market in Bergen

Market Square

The picturesque Fish Market in Bergen is one of Norway's most visited outdoors markets. A very popular activity is to buy freshly boiled shrimp and eat by the waterfront next to the stands at the Fish Market.

Famous food items people like in Bergen

SWEDEN

Bidding farewell to Oslo, we headed for Stockholm. Once we crossed the border into Sweden, the first surprise was to switch our driving from the right side to the left side of the road. Sweden was the country that did not change to driving on the right-hand side until 3 September 1967.

Stockholm

Stockholm City Hall *Drottningholm Palace UNESCO World Heritage*

This 17th century palace is now the official residence of the Swedish Royal Family. The pride of the Swedish Imperial fleet, the battleship *Vasa,* was launched in 1628, sank on its maiden voyage, but was salvaged. This medieval ship is a matter of national and historic pride. As far as Swedes are concerned, it is the greatest engineering feat of mankind. Or at least, medieval-kind.

In this trip to Sweden, I was able to pick up a few useful tips. When you are in Sweden, don't mention the Finnish ice hockey team. You support the Swedish Hockey team. End of story. This is the safest option, unless you want to start an argument. The Swedes and the Finns have a long and complex history, so anyone not from Sweden or Finland had best leave it at that. Swedes have fun, but just enough without making a nuisance of themselves. Remember that loud antagonizer at our local bar? You won't find it here.

I learned that highly animated body language is the quickest way to irritate the locals, and you can expect to be gently reprimanded if your voice carries over to the next table.

Vasa Museum

Sweden's most visited cathedral 1080

"Smorgasbord," meaning "many small dishes," is a Swedish buffet. It is a medley of different dishes such as hors d'oeuvres, hot and cold meats, smoked and pickled fish, cheeses, salads, and relishes. Pickled herring is placed at the centre of the smorgasbord. And I should mention that the Swedes are crazy for crayfish. Some of us love chocolate. Swedes love pickled herring.

Smoked fish like mackerel, eel and salmon is also popular. Fish smokeries in the villages along the coastline offer locally caught and smoked delicacies.

Smorgasbord *Fermented food*

A tradition since at least the 16th century: Surstromming, or Sour Baltic herring, one culinary specialty that makes both locals and visitors cringe - a stinky tradition. The custom preferably takes place outdoors owing to the overpowering, unpleasant smell, which many compare to rotten eggs and raw sewage. I must confess I was not brave enough to try this specialty.

In the Ferry to Finland, I met an American teaching high school for two years in Sweden and this is what I have learned: the Swedes are predominantly upper middle class, and they can boast they have the most far reaching social security system in the world. Perhaps visiting Sweden is a good time for a detox. If you enjoy a drink, you might want to stock up on duty free liquors en route to Sweden. Gas stations and local stores are forbidden to sell wine and hard liquors. In an effort to control alcohol consumption in the country, the government set up Systembolaget stores in 1955. The stores have a monopoly on retail sales of alcohol: it's the only place you can buy wine, spirits and beer with an alcohol content above 3.5 percent.

FINLAND

We took the 11 hr ferry night trip from Stockholm to Turku, Finland in the Baltic Sea. It was very relaxing and comfortable. During WWII we were told that this area was very dangerous due to the presence of German U boats. Finland was part of Sweden for almost 700 years from around 1150 until the Finnish War of 1809 that saw Finland becoming an autonomous part of Russia as the Grand Duchy of Finland. Since Finland gained its full independence from Russia in 1917, Finland and Russia have been close partners enjoying a Special Relationship. Don't compare Finland to other countries especially Sweden. Do not try to start a conversation by asking if Finland was once a communist country like its neighbouring Russia. It is like comparing Catholics to Protestants.

The number of Finnish-Swedish connections and the quality of cooperation in most areas of the government is unique when compared to the other international relations of both countries. Swedish language has an official status in Finland whilst Finns form the largest ethnic minority in Sweden, estimated to be about 675, 000.

Market Square, City Hall and Cathedral

Coming from Sweden, I had to switch again to driving on the right side. I learned that Suomi means Finland in the Finnish language. No wonder many streets in Helsinki have both Swedish and Finnish names. I even saw signs "school for Swedish only" in 1958!

Tuomiokirkko Lutheran Cathedral 1852

Uspenski Cathedral

I had the opportunity to visit the imposing Uspenski Eastern Orthodox Cathedral in Helsinki commemorating Emperor Alexander II of Russia, the sovereign of Finland in the 19th century. It's the largest Orthodox Church in Western Europe..

This particular Olympic Stadium was old and beautiful, built in the 1930s but not used until the 1950s to hold the Olympic Games. It was clean and had a very modern feel and look about it. The art deco design took care of that. It was not just the use of space and economy of design that gave this building a young fresh feel, it was the fact that it seemed like it had only just been built. The maintenance of the stadium was immaculate. It bore testimony to the Finnish attitude of keeping that which is beautiful and works. The tower once burned the flame of Olympic hope but now seduced a populace with its ageless youth.

The country's harsh climate meant that fresh fruit and vegetables were largely unavailable for nine months of the year, leading to a heavy reliance on staple tubers (initially turnip, later potato), and dark rye bread. Finnish restaurants offer a typical

Scandinavian smorgasbord. The world's best Russian restaurants can be found in Helsinki.

Fortress of Suomenlinna

Built in the second half of the 18th century by Sweden on a group of islands located at the entrance of Helsinki's harbour, this fortress is an especially interesting example of European military architecture of the time.

1. **iittala** *Finnish flatware of modern design*

2. **marimekko** *made important contributions to fashion, architecture*

World's famous iittala started as a glass factory in 1881, but the Finnish company's breakthrough came in the early years of modernism and functionalism during the '30s and '40s. Finland's **marimekko** & **iittala** are household names across the world. While in Helsinki, I applied for a visa to visit Saint Petersburg which was only 244 miles away. Russia required seven days to process my visa. I did not have much to do in Helsinki for a week and decided to return to Denmark to continue to visit Germany.

GERMANY

In Bavaria, the beer brewing tradition crafted in Munich over centuries is acclaimed throughout the entire world and celebrated with the Octoberfest festival among others. Beer is traditionally served by the liter! The purity law in 1487 allows only three ingredients in beer: water, barley, and hops. I enjoyed Munich very much, a city that just knows how to have fun. Anything Munich does, it does on a grand scale. Like its beer.

Munich Marienplatz, Bavaria

Beer and Food

Lady and eight one liter Beer mugs (steins)

Bratwurst

Sauerkraut   *Pickled Eisbein with Sauerkraut*

Nothing is a more authentic south German food than a delicious, fresh-from-the-oven soft pretzel.

1. Lentils and spätzle (noodles typical of Southern Germany).

2. Pretzel Münchner Weißwurst, a Bavarian sausage

We tried these dishes on a floating restaurant on the Rhine at Cologne and enjoyed also the German Riesling miracle.

Pschorr beer hall

Rhine river

Rhine and Moselle at Coblentz

Watching the scenery where the Rhine meets the Moselle at Coblentz I felt it's a journey worth taking in its own right. A glass of crisp white Riesling is authentic through and through. I was surprised to see castles at every turn of the Moselle.

Cologne Cathetral

Munich Frauenkirche Church and Town hall

The city is home of world famous Eau de Cologne with a particular scent that's been produced here since 1792.

AUSTRIA

Vista panoramic of Salzburg with its fortress

Salzburg was the birthplace of 18th-century composer Amadeus Mozart and major celebrations take place throughout the year to attract tourists.

Mozart birthplace at Getreidegasse 9

Tanzmeisterhaus, the Mozart family residence dating to 1773

Innsbruck

Vienna City Hall, or Rathaus

Vienna State Opera

In September 1958 parts of the Hofburg were opened to the public as a convention center.

Goldenes Dachl - Famous landmark in Innsbruck

Mozartplatz with Mozart Statue

Apfelstrudel, a Viennese speciality

Wiener schnitzel consisting of a thin slice of veal coated in breadcrumbs and fried.

Vienna has so many monuments that reminded me of the city of Paris. It is known for its coffee, patisserie Viennoise and historical architecture. Recently, for the fourth consecutive year, Vienna has been ranked as the number one city with the highest quality of life in the world, surpassing cities in Switzerland, Denmark, and the U.S. The title was bestowed by Mercer, a global consulting firm. This is a big surprise for me because I have lived for more than 40 years in San Francisco and coming from a "chopstick culture" I find San Francisco more appealing with mild climate, high air quality, world-class restaurants, museums, community fairs and music festivals, large educated class, and a high-tech economy with nearby Google, Yahoo, Facebook, HP, Intel, Cisco, eBay, Oracle, Netflix, Apples…

SWITZERLAND

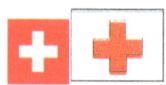

For me, when I first arrived in Switzerland, I had the impression that the Swiss had a gentle but perceptible air of superiority. For over 675 years, Switzerland has maintained her status as an independent nation – no small feat for a nation in the heart of Europe. *From my 1948 school days in Lycée Yersin Dalat, Vietnam, my French geography professor Mr. Convert taught me about the Swiss's flag vs the Red Cross, the country's three major languages German, French and Italian, Swiss famous chocolate, cheese, watches, cowbell, Army knife, alphorn…and last but not least t*he Protestant Church of Geneva was founded in 1536 *by the Frenchman Jean Calvin.*

Now visiting the country for the first time I had my chance to see the famous "Jet d'Eau" installed in 1951, a fountain with a near-500 foot-high water jet in Lake

Geneva, an icon of the city of Genève. It's so high that later, on my Pan Am flight from Paris to Milan, I could see it from the plane's window. During my tour in Lausanne, I had the pleasure of tasting Swiss cheese fondue. The bread cubes were picked up with a fork and swivelled in the melted Gruyere and Emmenthaler cheeses, which were served in a traditional ceramic fondue pot called 'caquelon.'

Swiss fondue

"Jet d'Eau" on Lake Geneva

Swiss life, as Swiss food, has been very much influenced by its neighbors: France, Germany, Austria, and Italy. Specialty dishes from each of these countries have long been intertwined with local regional tastes. With world tourism, the Swiss have attempted more exotic fare adapted from Chinese cooking but retaining mildness in flavor.

I observed that class structure is not particularly visible. The middle class was large and for its members, upward or downward social mobility seemed rather easy. Not like in New York, to manifest a demonstration of wealth was negatively valued here, but poverty was perceived as shameful, and many people seemed to hide their economic situation. Kindness and politeness in social interaction were expected; in smaller shops, clients and vendors thanked each other several times.

The alphorn

Zurich

Lausanne Cathedral

Chocolate

Chocolate was processed in Switzerland in the 17th century. Swiss troops had a reputation for discipline and loyalty, and for employing revolutionary battle tactics such as the pike square.

Nowadays, the name Swiss Guard generally refers to the Pontifical Swiss Guard of the Holy See stationed at the Vatican in Rome. The Papal Swiss Guard has a bodyguard-like role.

ITALY

From calm Switzerland, I passed to a more turbulent Italy. There was more body language; life seemed to be more exciting. The food became more interesting. Security wise, it was not as safe as in the North. In fact, I had a bad experience in a shop. While selecting some souvenirs, I lost my beautiful silk ties gift box just bought next door. I saw frequently signs "beware of pick pockets" something unthinkable in Northern Europe. There was surely the matter of Anglo-Saxon vs Latin Temperament.

Rome Colosseum

Milan cathedral

Italy has become home to the greatest number of UNESCO World Heritage Sites in the world. High art and monuments are to be found everywhere around the country. Its great cities of art, like Rome, Venice and Florence are world famous. However, because of limited time, I had to choose only a few places to visit.

Florence's Basilica di Santa Maria del Fiore

Venice

Panorama of Assisi

Assisi was the birthplace of St. Francis, who founded the Franciscan religious order in the town in 1208; it's a Sister City of San Francisco, USA.

Pisa tower

Italian food

Unlike faster paced societies of the world, meal time in Italy is a time to kick back and relax. I enjoyed a lot of fettuccini with sauces and green tomato salad in the summer.

Pizza Margherita, spaghetti alla carbonara, gelato and espresso.

I have remembered that Gelato, tiramisu and patisserie are among the most famous examples of Italian desserts. The Mediterranean diet forms the basis of Italian cuisine, rich in pasta, fish, fruits and vegetables and characterized by its extreme simplicity and variety.

BACK TO PARIS

I finally completed my very demanding 15, 000 km tour of Western Europe. Being a little exhausted, I decided to "stay home," relax and enjoy the City of Light before boarding the Pan Am flight for Saigon. I was looking for some of my Vietnamese classmates from Dalat Lycée Yersin who were studying in France. One of my buddies Vĩnh Mậu became a brilliant nuclear physicist from the University of Paris. He took me to a special restaurant "Au Cochon de Lait » near Notre Dame de Paris. The quality of food was very high. In the evening it was very enjoyable to walk along the Seine watching the "bateaux mouches" or sit at the sidewalk café looking at the happy summer tourists.

The City of Light *Cafés on the boulevard St. Michel in the Latin Quarter*

Seine river and bateau mouche

Street life and sidewalk café near the Seine

The Louvre with controversial glass pyramid by MIT architect I.M. Pei

Basilique-Sacré Cœur   *Arc de Triomphe*

My twin brother Khương Hữu Quí was a student in Paris since 1951. He finished his pharmacy degree in 1956 and continued toward his Ph.D. in Sciences. He was living in my sister Chị Ba Khuê's comfortable apartment in Parc Montsouris. We enjoyed special French gourmet popular dishes paired with good wines. I remember walking with him one night on a very dark, quiet street. When we entered into the only restaurant in the area, we found to our surprise, a noisy, well lighted place full of happy customers; the specialty was just a kidney dish. Truly it was delicious. Regularly, we simply enjoyed the popular "bistros du coin" with Pâté de campagne, Escargots à la Bourguignonne, Grilled steak with french fries and Béarnaise sauce, White bean stew with sausage, pork, lamb and duck confit, Magret de canard au poivre vert, Pêche Melba, Apple tart with Calvados.

Of course, we took the Seine river boat to see Paris by night. Finally, well rested, I continued my journey home by Pan Am flight from Paris to Milan, Athens, Cairo, Teheran, Bombay, New Delhi, Calcutta, Rangoon, Bangkok, Phnom-Penh and Saigon!

GREECE

When I was in Athens in 1958, the city was dusty and noisy with traffic jams because Greece was modernizing its cities for world's tourism.

I was totally amazed watching the Parthenon which is viewed as an enduring symbol of Ancient Greece and of Athenian democracy. It is regarded as one of the world's greatest cultural monuments.

Greek traditional dance

Zeus temple in Athens

My Lafayette schoolmate, Tony Antonopoulos has asked me to stop and see his mother in Athens. I had a chance to talk to her about our life at Lafayette College. She and her daughter took me to a popular restaurant near the waterfront for a treat of local dishes: grilled octopus and lamb kabab. I have tried also these popular specialities: Dolmades (stuffed vine leaves), Moussaka (aubergine casserole with minced lamb, cinnamon, red wine and olive oil), Calamari (deep-fried rings of squid) or htapodia (octopus), Horiatiki (Greek salad: feta cheese, tomato, cucumber, green peppers, black Kalamata olives and fresh olive oil) paired with Ouzo (an aniseed-based clear spirit to which water was added)

Greek Feta salad

Roasted lamb

I was told that lamb is preferred on the mainland and goat on the islands. They are slow roasted on the spit or buried in the ground with charcoals.

Octopus sun-dried before grilling   *Marinated octopus*

Greek cookery, historically a forerunner of Western cuisine, spread its culinary influence – via ancient Rome – throughout Europe and beyond. It was characterized by its frugality and was founded on the "Mediterranean triad" wheat, olive oil and wine with meat being rare and fish being more common.

I took a bus to Corinth to see its famous ruins. I was surprised to find a well-preserved ten-century old bible in a regular church glass case. Thanks to a very beautiful weather. People dried grapes on the sides of the streets to make raisins. I have learned that Greece was the birthplace of Western culture and democracy. It was the Greeks who created the ideal of beauty that strongly influenced Western art.

Temple in Corinth   *Oldest known grapes, Corinth*

Something new to me: the letter Swastika from ancient Greek culture has been used as a symbol of good fortune, the universe and at a later date Buddhism. It is also a symbol cherished and revered in numerous cultures through eons in human history. During the 20th century, Hitler and the Nazis took this sacred symbol, the symbol of the Buddha, and twisted it to serve their own corrupt and evil agenda.

EGYPT

Pyramids and camel ride

The Pyramids and the Sphinx

From the Cairo Nile Hilton I took a bus to see the Pyramids and the Sphinx. In 1958 there were fewer tourists. I accepted to crawl inside the narrow tunnel toward the interior of the Pyramid with butterflies in my stomach. Then I rode a camel. It was a much rougher ride than I expected. On the way back to the Hilton, one completely unknown Egyptian colonel contacted me and said that he just came back from Beijing and would like to invite me to his home for more conversation. Obviously he thought I was Chinese. I was just a lucky guy. My MIT class ring has helped. I appreciated the warm hospitality of this Egyptian family. We walked along the Nile and I found street vendors grilling sweet corn on the cob on hot charcoal, exactly like in Saigon. What a nostalgic scene! In the evening, his father treated us a good curry dinner with goat testicles, a gourmet dish in Cairo. By the way, Egyptians eat pigeon like we eat chicken. No wonder you could see pigeon cages on most of the roofs in town.

Stuffed Pigeon   *Koshary*

Also remember that Koshary is considered one of the most famous dishes in Egypt. This vegetarian meal contains rice, spaghetti, macaroni, black lentils, chick peas, garlic, and is topped with a spicy tomato sauce and fried onions. You will find Koshary being sold cheaply at street stalls and also in restaurants, some only specializing in this dish. So basically, you can't leave Egypt without trying this.

Typical fūl medames breakfast as served by an Egyptian street vendor with bread and pickled vegetables, as well as fresh arugula leaves on the side

Egyptian Museum

Coffin of King Tut in the Egyptian museum   *The Gold Mask of Tutankhamun*

The golden throne of Tutankhamun

Interior of Egyptian museum in Cairo2

Coptic Museum in Cairo

IRAN

Shah of Iran and Soraya, 1958

In Persian, the word Iran means "Land of the Aryans." In 1958 the Shah was in power in Iran. Now the official name of Iran is the Islamic Republic of Iran. It became an Islamic republic in 1979 when the Shah was overthrown and religious clerics assumed political power under supreme leader Ayatollah Khomeini.

Teheran

Pan Am booked a room for me at the Teheran Hilton located in the European part of the city. As a tourist, I preferred to venture into the so called native Iranian quarter. Coming from New York, it was quite a surprise to see a town full of women covered in black Hijabs, the Islamic dress-code, with only the eyes visible behind a veil.

Types of clothes worn by Muslims   *"Hijabs" conceals the hair and neck*

Normally the maximum penalty for disregarding the Hijab rule is a request by police or authorities to make it correct.

Teheran

Hilton1958

Many tourists I met at the Hilton had prepared their trips well. They suggested that I should visit Esfahan, Shiraz and Persepolis to appreciate the rich culture of Iran. In 1971, the Shah had a great project to celebrate in Persepolis the 2,500th anniversary of the founding of the Iranian monarchy (Persian Empire) by Cyrus the Great. The intent of the celebration was to demonstrate Iran's long history and to showcase its contemporary advancements under the Shah of Iran. Later in 1971, I saw some parts of the $200 million Festival on TV. Six hundred guests dined over five and a half hours in the desert thus making for the longest and most lavish official banquet in modern history as recorded by the Guinness Book of World Records.

Tent City in the desert

Guests' tents in the desert

Cyrus's Mausoleum 4th century BC

Isfahan

I did pay a visit to the city nicknamed "Isfahan is half the World." It is perhaps Iran's best known touristic city. Naqsh-e Jahan Square, a square at the center of the city, is also a world heritage site.

Naqsh-e Jahan Square, 430km south of Teheran

Due to its beautiful hand-painted tiling and magnificent Public Square, it is considered to be one of the most beautiful cities in the world.

1. *An Iranian woman dressed in a chador inside Sheikh Lotfollah Mosque*
2. *Conjunction of the Moon and Venus as seen from the World Heritage Site of Naqsh-e Jahan square (meaning "Picture of the World")*

The dome of the Imam mosque   *Blue arch of a mosque*

There was no skyscraper and the mosques dominated the famous Iranian cities.

Shiraz
(Capital of Persia from 1598 to 1722)

Eram garden

The Eram garden (Garden of Paradise) in Shiraz is a typical Persian garden. Shiraz is the city of love, Persian poetry, and home to many touristic sites. Within a relatively short driving distance from Shiraz are the ruins of Persepolis, city of poets, gardens, flowers and the nightingale.

Shah Cheragh mosque 1130s AD

The mosque is the most important place of pilgrimage within the city of Shiraz.

Mosques in Shiraz

Persepolis

Aerial view of Persepolis

I took a taxi to see the ruins of Persepolis, not far from Shiraz. Persepolis was the capital of the Achaemid Empire and one of the world's most magnificient ancient sites. It was declared a world heritage site in 1979 by UNESCO.

Panorama of the ruins of Persepolis, 6th century BC

Ruins of the Gate of All Nations   *"Two head Bull"*

1. The Apadana, great audience hall
2. The stairs of Apadana Palace, Persepolis about 500 BC

Food: I remember each time Air France made a stop at Teheran airport, I ran fast to the airport food counter to buy duty free Iranian caviar. Many times, the Air France crew emptied the caviar shelf before the passengers' arrival.

Iranian caviars

Many other coveted food items are native to Iran, including pistachios, almonds, walnuts, saffron, mint, oranges, and pomegranates.

I found a stunning variety of culinary delights. What surprised me most was the street merchants selling everywhere in town nothing but lettuce with local vinaigrette as snack. I was thinking of this ancient culture with such advanced knowledge of healthy nutrition. Iranian cuisine and Turkish cuisine have marked mutual influence on each other, due to geographical proximity and ethnic relations.

The Persian Kabab is served with rice   *pilaf*

1.A bowl of soup made with pomegranates
2.A simple rice dish, Baghdadi Polo is made with saffron, green dill and fava beans 3.Jeweled Rice (Rice with Nuts and Dried Fruit)

Grilled lamb's testicles   *Person Dolma (Stuffed Grape Leaves)*

The traditional drink is a combination of yogurt, carbonated or plain water, salt, and dried mint. There are certain accompaniments essential to every Iranian lunch and dinner. These include a plate of fresh herbs (basil, cilantro, coriander, fenugreek, green onion, mint, radish, savory tarragon, and Persian watercress), a variety of flat breads, fresh white cheese, walnuts, sliced and peeled cucumbers, sliced tomatoes, yogurt and lemon juice. Tea is served at breakfast. Stew over rice is a popular dish.

INDIA

Bombay: Gate of India

I had a very pleasant surprise flying Air India from Cairo to Bombay. I talked to the captain about my interest in jet planes as a mechanical engineer from MIT. My class ring seemed to confirm my interest. He was so kind to invite me to the cockpit to show me a few interesting items on the control board of the turbo-prop Viscount plane, something unheard of in these days of Islamic terrorism! In 1958, airline passengers were treated with courtesy. It was real fun to see from the cockpit the lights of big cities below at night.

1. Street colors in Bombay
2. Old Taj hotel
3. New Taj-Mahal-palace-hotel

1. Old Bombay - Crawford Market
2. Clock tower
3. Mount Mary Church

Like the French in Vietnam, the British built many prestigious, monuments in their Empire for showing-off.

When I walked away from the majestic monument centers and got closer to where the majority of the people lived, then things looked very different. I saw everywhere in town the monkey menace that destroyed trees and ram into moving vehicles causing serious damage to human life and property. Bombay's 30,000 unruly monkeys steal stuff, terrorize people and even kill. I was shocked by what I had never seen before in my life. Cow and monkey are considered sacred. The consequences are beyond my imagination. There is a new profession in Indians using langurs to solve government problems. A langur is a bully monkey. He has three-inch canines that glisten when he snarls. He's able to scare off this city's 30,000 smaller, red-faced rhesus monkeys and in the process to protect the local human population from their naughty and dangerous antics. In the 21st century, the Indian government still pays owners of langurs to deploy them in government buildings to police primates that harass the bureaucrats by stealing their files and food.

1. A langur sits on a New Delhi Municipal Council truck, transported to a stadium to scare away smaller rhesus monkeys
2. Langur monkeys stand on leashes held by their owners in front of the Commonwealth
3. Langur monkeys follow their handler at the forecourt of India's presidential palace Rashtrapati Bhavan in New Delhi

1. India employs men in ape suits to drive away Parliament's monkeys
2. Monkeys cross the road in front of India's Presidential Palace
3. Monkeys play on highways.

In 2007, New Delhi's deputy mayor, Surinder Singh Bajwa, fell from his terrace and died after being attacked by monkeys at his home. In 2015, I saw on TV, monkeys occupying the New Delhi Defense Department computer room and the government hired owners of langurs to chase the monkeys away. The problems I saw in 1958 caused by religion remain unchanged in 2016. Cows create similar problems in modern India. Killing or smuggling a cow is equivalent to raping a Hindu girl.

Indian woman sprinkles yogurt paste onto a cow's forehead during a Hindu ritual to bless the animal.

City Centre: Cows routinely blocking street

Food: I remember well the seven Bombay textile shops in Mỹ Tho, my hometown in the Mekong Delta. The Indians held the monopoly of textiles imported from Bombay. Our family cook "Thiếm Tư" used to work for a rich Indian in town. So, at home, I ate a lot of good Indian curries. It was now time for me to taste the real Indian curry in Bombay. My first observation was the cheap labor in India. I counted 11 uniformed waiters serving me in this middle-class restaurant. Of course, I tried the native "hot curry." I had another shock. Even for Indians, the dish was served with a bowl of very bitter juice to neutralize the burning of the palate!

1. Hearty Indian goat curry, goat vindaloo (Bombay style), with naan, basmati rice and creamy sauce
2. Tandoori Chicken

My Indian friends took me to an outdoor restaurant for Tandoori chicken.

Tandoory clay oven

Calcutta prawn curry

Lamb Curry Calcutta

Spicy goat meat curry

New Delhi

My next stop was New Delhi. I was lucky to have met a few young Indian students who volunteered to be my guides.

The Red Fort

The Red Fort

In 1638 Shahjahan transferred his capital from Agra to Delhi and laid the foundations of Shahjahanabad, the seventh city of Delhi enclosed by a rubble stone wall, with bastions, gates and wickets at intervals. The Red Fort was the residence of the Mughal emperor of India for nearly 200 years, until 1857. It is now located in the center of Delhi and houses a number of museums.

1. 5-story victory tower, Qutub Minar, 1369 standing still in spite of the ages
2. The lantern that used to be at the top, today in the garden
3. 1600-year old Iron Pillar located in Delhi

Humayun's tomb is the tomb of the Mughal Emperor Humayun in Delhi 1569, designed by a Persian architect, "The other Taj Mahal worth seeing."

India Gate: 1920s Triumphal Arch

India Gate is a symbol of India built to commemorate the Indian Army soldiers who died in the First World War.

Jantar Mantar – Built in 1724 by Maharaja Jai Singh II of Jaipur, the Jantar Mantar consists of 13 architectural astronomy instruments. Today Jantar Mantar is one of the most visited tourist attractions in Delhi owing to its unique architecture and historical significance.

The Scientific Wonder Jantar Mantar

The Jama Masjid of Delhi is one of the largest mosques in India, 1656

Chandni Chowk, home of delicious and cheap eats!

Crowded street of New Delhi

Cooking naan in a tandoori oven

Naan is a type of flat bread cooked in a tandoori clay oven. I have to admit that the place was dirty but the food was really delicious and cheap.

I saw many beggars in town. On the streets of Old Delhi, one would be forced to hand out money very often. In the face of overwhelming poverty, it was not easy not to give when I saw a young boy sitting in the gutter minus a foot. Most tourists visiting New Delhi took a 3 hour train to Agra to see the world famous and beautiful Taj Mahal.

Taj Mahal

Taj Mahal

The Taj Mahal, 1632, is a mausoleum located in Agra, built by Mughal emperor Shah Jahan in memory of his favorite wife, Mumtaz Mahal. It is the jewel of Muslim art in India and one of the universally admired masterpieces of the world's UNESCO Heritage Center.

Stunning beauty of the interior of the Taj mahal

Calcutta

Before I landed in Calcutta , I had been warned by friends that the City was one of the poorest megapolises in India. Sure enough, for the first time in my life I saw four bodies starving to death on the sides of the street. There were a lot of unsettling things in India. Please be ready for something scary and unthinkable for a tourist: I saw the body of a young woman being burned on a funeral pyre, and afterwards the dogs snuffling through the ashes and running off with morsels of meat. The sheer in-your-face starkness of the whole place combined with the manic religious devotion that forms a part of everyday life force you to face up to who you believe yourself to be. Yes, India is life with the volume turned up very high. I also met sadhus - holy men - who had forsaken material life and devoted themselves to asceticism. I saw the bullet holes in buildings where British colonial soldiers had massacred Sikhs. Many visitors will be overwhelmed by the garbage, rivers that are often putrid with sewage and air that is yellow with dust. Though there is a business center in Calcutta, the city has many slums.

Many slums

1. Workers take an afternoon siesta on a sidewalk
2. Polluted street

1. Polluted river
2. Calcutta's plants suffer from power cuts and monkeys

I could not believe my ears when I heard about a temple for rats in the city. I thought only monkeys and cows are sacred not rats.

1. Temple where rats are treated with kindness and a regular bowl of milk
2. Rat carvings on front door

This Shri Karni Mata Temple is unlike any other Hindu temple in the world. In this temple, rats reign supreme.

The Victoria Memorial

Dakshineswar Kali Temple 1847

National library

Writer's Building

Facade of the Calcutta High Court

Town Hall

The British have left, like in other cities, many imposing buildings for the prestige of the British Empire. The French have done the same in Indochina.

In summary of the two dozen countries I visited in this long trip, India with Bombay, Calcutta and New Delhi gave me the most shocking surprises. The physical conditions of Calcutta are appalling, simultaneously noble and squalid. The city has a highly successful professional class, while millions of its citizens still live in abject poverty.

Many of India's problems arise from the sheer size of its population: 433,000,000 in 1958 and 1,330,000,000 in 2016. In any picture of modern India, it is impossible to leave out religion and the caste system with its inevitable discrimination. In times past, one imagines, the problem would not have existed as all waste would consist of such material as banana skins, crushed sugar cane, wood carvings and vegetable waste. This would be routinely tossed out into the streets where the famous holy cows would devour the majority of it (surely the real reason why these beasts are allowed to roam freely). Whatever was left would be swept up by the untouchables, put into carts and dumped into the nearest river, pond or creek. This practice doesn't seem to have changed much except that nowadays, industrial waste is full of plastics.

Anyway, for all the talk of India becoming an advanced industrial nation like the US or European countries I say: no way. That will never be. The limiting factors that reflect the scale of the problems she faces are just too constrictive. Any tourist who sits beside the Ganges long enough will see locals using the river as both bath and toilet and note the steady stream of waste flowing past, including the remnants of funerals and rituals, as well as dead and bloated animals, all swirling by in the tug of the river's muddy waters. Poverty in India takes many forms: poverty in energy, poverty of the environment, poverty of knowledge, poverty in skills, and above all for a democratic country like India, poverty in political life.

BURMA
(Myanmar)

Rangoon

Land of the Golden Spires

My next stop was Rangoon, Burma whose name was changed to Yangon, Myanmar in 1989 by the ruling Military Junta. Rangoon was a British colonial city with some similarities with Saigon. My hotel looked like the Majestic hotel in Saigon: four huge-blade fans in the ceiling as "the old-style air conditioning."

Shwedagon Pagoda

Almost anywhere in town I could see the tall, majestic Shwedagon Pagoda, the most sacred and impressive Buddhist site for the people of Burma. The 2,500 year-old temple enshrined strands of Buddha's hair and other holy relics.

Old Rangoon

Rangoon street

Many Buddhist monks seen in town

Buddhist novice monks walk to collect alms and offerings in town. This procession is held every morning.

Telegraph office in downtown

To my big surprise, I saw many Burmese women and teenagers smoked locally made cigars, and that children bear the mother's last name. The matrilineal communities have family names inherited from their mothers. At a social gathering, you will often find that the Burmese women cluster together on one side of the room and leave their men to talk to each other in a group of their own. On the street there is nothing unusual if you see a man walking ahead while his wife follows a few paces behind carrying the bundles. I am talking about 1958. Of course, things are different in 2016 with many thanks to Mrs. Aung San Suu Kyi, a Burmese politician and president of Myanmar's National League for Democracy (NLD), the party that won the recent national election.

In the 50's, the Burmese government sent Mr. U Thant to the United Nations to serve as its Ambassador. He later became the third Secretary General of that body.

U Thant, Secretary General of the UN.

Food in Rangoon

I went from one surprise to another. Many dishes are almost the same as in Thailand or China.

Crab Curry

Steamed live red grouper

Breakfast like Chinese Dim Sum

Shrimp covered in fried garlic!

Vegetable market

THAILAND

Bangkok

The Ananta Samakhom Throne Hall was inspired by King Chulalongkorn's visits to Europe

Grand Palace

Oriental hotel

Pan Am chose for me the old Oriental hotel with river terrace gazing out at the Chao Phraya River. Jim Thompson, the American who later made a name for himself in Thai silk, became one of the owners of the Oriental and its resident as well.

Jim Thompson house, founder of Thai Silk

World famous Thai silk

Bangkok 1958

Gourmet Thai crispy chicken wings   *The red curry chicken*

Shrimps wrapped in crispy bacon

Bangkok's Chinatown is a great place to sample some street food, and is arguably Bangkok's street food center.

Stewed pork legs and knuckles

Delicious juices and smoothies, all freshly made!

Floating markets

The city grew rapidly during the 1950s through the 1980s and now exerts a significant impact on Thailand's politics, economy, education, media and modern society.

CAMBODIA

Phnom Penh

Angkor Wat

Great Tonle Sap Lake

My next and last stop before arriving in Saigon was Phnom Penh. Instead of staying there to visit the world-famous Angkor Wat, I decided to continue straight home because of my rush to see my parents, my brother and sisters… Besides Cambodia was only one hour away from Saigon and I would surely have my chance to visil it in the near future. The reality was I could not see Angkor Wat at all because the war in Indochina continued nonstop to April 30, 1975! During the refueling stop at Pochentong International Airport I had the opportunity to see for the first time the Air Cambodia commercial Russian Tupolev plane. As a mechanical engineer, I found it very crude with characteristics of a cargo rather than a passenger carrier.

When my DC-4 took off for Saigon, I was watching curiously every mile on my way back to my homeland after seven years of absence. I was impressed by the huge Tonle Sap Lake commonly translated to mean the "Grand Lake" of the lower Mekong basin, the largest freshwater lake in Southeast Asia. It's an important food source for Cambodia and Vietnam. The jungle between Phnom Penh and Saigon was so thick that I could not see anything but the green color of the tropical forest. After only 30 minutes, the plane started to descend to Tân Sơn Nhứt airport. Thank God for the long awaited happy and emotional family reunion.

CONCLUSION

I want to remind my readers that in this book "EAST meets WEST," I have a lot of observations and surprises from my trips in 1958 that may be obvious to most Americans and Europeans but may be all new to a lot of Asians. However even for someone who has seen the world, who is very familiar with all these places, it may still make for interesting reading and brings back great memories. And I did not want to miss anything!

I asked myself what had I learned after 90 days of seeing 23 countries in a tour of about 15,000 km of Western Europe and another 15,000 km by Pan Am from Paris to Saigon. Along the way, I have really acquired many interesting lessons useful for the rest of my life. *The Vietnamese have a saying: "Đi một ngày đàng, học một sàng khôn."*

Literally: "Travel for a day, get a full tray of knowledge"

After more than thirty years of outdoor experience in the Western States of America, I see many differences in camping between Europe and the States. The vast New World has plenty of spacious supernatural sites to build campgrounds in national, regional, states and county parks. In Europe, after thousands of years of development, there is limited wilderness land mass left except probably in Siberia. Camping in the United States is more for enjoying outdoor life with Nature than for financial gain or saving. I was a little surprised to see much fewer middle class campers during my 15,000 km tour and very few comfortable mobile home in the 50's. The real objective of the campgrounds owned by the federal and local governments is not for commercial exploitation. Most of them have spacious campsites with even line fence around each site for campers' privacy. Many campgrounds have safe drinking water, flush toilets and hot showers. In Canada, campers often get free firewood from rangers at the campsite! In 1958, all the super highways in the West were toll free and gasoline was cheap. I met many retired people with luxurious mobile homes i.e. with TV, air conditioning, Jacuzzi, bar dining room, flush toilet and hot showers. They spent many months of outdoor per year. In Europe, I noticed that most camp sites were smaller and provided fewer amenities. I felt lucky to have known many years of super natural outdoor living.

In Scandinavia, I learned a lot on how to design my future home in Vietnam with modern, functional ideas in architecture, interior design, landscaping, etc.… Finland's world famous *iitali's* porcelain and glasses collections embody design, which is characterized by natural, clear forms and high functionality. It's Simplicity and Timeless Design.

One of the greatest contrasts seemed to be the difference between Scandinavia and Southwest Asia. It was my impression that the much colder climate in the North was responsible for the completely different supply of food and ingredients compared to those of tropical countries: our rice vs wheat bread; exotic spices as the source of our very hot and spicy dishes. The cold pickled fish type and cold milk for breakfast was unheard of because of our usual boiling hot pho noodles or congees with hot tea and coffee. For the first time in the 50's, I ate a lot of blue whale and reindeer steaks. In Vietnam people built altars and tombs for dead whales at their beaches!

I noticed also some main differences between the two groups Anglo-Saxons-Scandinavian vs Latin Europe (France, Spain, Portugal, Italy).

Home facilities were much more comfortable up north with better sanitary conditions. The gap between rich and poor was tolerable with the "tenderloin" section of town not as miserable or repulsive as in many parts of Southeast Asia. In architecture, I liked the simple, clean line design of the buildings. For instance, the City Halls in Oslo, Stockholm, and Helsinki gave me good examples of simple streamlined concept vs the more elaborate styles of those in Southern Europe.

I saw some interesting and surprising overlapping similarities in architecture and design between the Japanese and the Scandinavian. It's Simplicity and Timeless Design.

Southern European life style appeared to be more exciting than the Anglo-Saxon one. The Latin characteristics seemed to be more flamboyant, gastronomy spicier and more time consuming. They spent more time for their meals. You would find more body language in the South.

It happened more than half a century ago but I often reminisce about that long trip home from New York. It was my last chance to travel while still overseas. I had already learned a lot of good things during my seven years stay in America but that Western Europe and the World tour really opened my eyes and made me appreciate fuller my own life. I became a more rounded human being. The travel helped me acquire good judgment and developed skills that I didn't know I had.

One of the best things about that trip was that I learned so much from exploring foreign lands, knowing different kinds of people with their particular cultures, foods and ways of life. It surely influenced me in my way of thinking and feeling about life. I then realized that, deep inside, I have been able to accommodate myself into the American "Melting Pot" and have successfully blended my "Eastern traditions and customs" with "Western values."

It must also be said that in the 1950's there were very few Vietnamese who had the opportunity of staying seven long years in America and traveling through Western Europe as I did with my 90-day world tour home to Saigon. Thank God for giving me a break or opportunity to learn about the world at the start of my career. In this way those early lessons in life have continued to help me for more than half a century later.

CHAPTER 10

My Life in Saigon from 1958-1975

Home after my first 7-year stay in the U.S.

Saigon at much slower pace than New York City!

Tree lined street with tropical blossoms   *People in a hurry all of the time*

After seven years of living in America, it was truly a thrill to be reunited with my family back in Saigon, Vietnam. The old Tân Sơn Nhứt Airport had not changed much during my absence. The terminal was so small that the minute I got out of the plane, I could see immediately my extended family members waving from the second floor on the roof terrace of the air terminal.

Tân Sơn Nhứt Airport   *Downtown with Continental Hotel at center of photo*

It was really an unforgettable family reunion filled with strong emotions. On the way from the airport to my new residence in Saigon, I observed that the old horse drawn carriages, the multitudes of motorcycles, the familiar blue & ivory color Renault 4CV taxis, and the tree-lined streets with flamboyant flowers, all were still there. (See photos)

Saigon with local modes of transportation, a great contrast with New York

National Assembly building at center of photo

Along some heavy traffic arteries, I noted that the old, tall trees had a hard time to survive in the bluish polluted air. In contrast to the rapid transit system of New York, Saigon, without the subway, offered a much slower transportation mode. There was no commuter rush like in Manhattan. However, local drivers abused too much the car horn, creating unpleasant noise pollution.

More exotic horse-drawn carriage with bus and taxi in one spot

From enclosed to open-air tricycles, to jeep, to Renault 4CV taxis

In the evening of my return, my father and I went to the famous Continental Hotel restaurant on Tự Do Street for a cozy tête-à-tête dinner. Saigon, traditionally known as the Pearl of the Extreme-Orient, had the best French food in Southeast Asia. It was a unique, emotional and unforgettable dinner between father and son after a long separation. For this occasion, he made a special trip from our hometown, Mỹ Tho, 70 km away, to welcome me home. It was the summit milestone of my youth: a very happy and moving reunion with my friendly father. He had an open secret and a pleasant surprise for me. He showed me the very popular monthly magazine "Gia Đình" or "Family" published by Saigon USIS (United States Information Service.) In it was a full-page article with great photos talking about my success as valedictorian at Lafayette College in Mechanical Engineering in 1956. (See photo below)

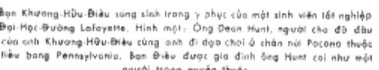

DU HỌC-SINH VIỆT-NAM TẠI MỸ

Translation of the above Vietnamese magazine article:

"Friend Khương Hữu Diểu in his school uniform as graduate student of the Lafayette College. Photo 1: Dean of Students Hunt, Khương Hữu Điểu's godfather, having an enjoyable stroll with him at the foot of the Pocono Mountains in the State of Pennsylvania. The family of Dean Hunt considered Điểu as a member of their own.

A student from Viet Nam, Khương Hữu Điểu pursued his engineering studies in the United States for over the past four years. Last year, Điểu was the most outstanding student and valedictorian of his class in mechanical engineering at Lafayette College at Easton, Pennsylvania. Điểu said: "When I return to my homeland, I will apply the American methods to the Vietnamese industrial sector but at the same time preserve the Asian culture of the country. I very much hope that my country will develop and improve robustly its industrial activities. We need equipment and, once back home, I will try to explain and propagate the American technology and methods of mechanization so that the technicians of my country know how to use them.

Viet Nam had plans to develop a network of hydroelectric power. Điểu looked forward to the early realization of such projects and hoped that later on he would be able to work at these locations. According to Điểu, a large amount of capital was needed for the hydropower projects. If possible, this amount of capital could come from the industrialists themselves and/or from the government.

Điểu also stressed: "I pay much attention to the smaller industrial sector. I will write an exposé about the foundry activities because presently Viet Nam does not have any such plant of meaningful scale operating with scientific methods. People can now see only small factories for cast iron as a family and handicraft business. I hope to see large factories working with engineering methods in the steel and cast iron sector."

Điểu also informed us that at home he had lived with his family and all the living expenses had been taken care of by his parents. For the moment, he was devoting all his efforts to his studies so that later on he would be able to serve his country with his acquired knowledge. During vacation times, he tried to find jobs to do, such as swimming instructor for the youngsters at the summer camps in Maine. With his earnings, he could do some tourism, travel here and there to have a better understanding of the American way of life. While teaching swimming to the youngsters, he was also able to learn some colloquial English from them. He visited with them the White Mountains in New Hampshire. In his contacts with the American youth, he could see that they had all the conditions to develop their minds and spirits as well as the facilities to improve the material aspects of their lives."

oOo

Thanks to my generous brother Five, I had a real decent "soft landing" in Saigon. He let me stay at a nice villa that he owned at 83 Ngô Thời Nhiệm Street, in a calm, beautiful residential neighborhood of the 3rd district in Saigon. There I lived with my cousin, Khương Hữu Hối a pharmacist, for the next two years; the time that was needed for me to finish fixing my own new home. My cousin and I were both single. We had been schoolmates at the Lycée Yersin in Dalat from 1948 to 1951: he was in the Philosophy branch and I was in the Mathematics branch.

Most of the time, middle class families had full-time cooks. We were fortunate to have a talented, retired chef from the French Lines sailing between Saigon and Marseille. We were served French gourmet food practically every day, quite a change from my regular meals on campus or in New York City.

My brother Five was very happy and proud of my academic achievements at MIT. As a reward for my success, he let me use his new agave color French Peugeot 403, with the license plate number NBR-081. I mention the license plate number because in Saigon, the plate # 9 (0+8+1) was a very desirable sign of good luck. I began working at the ESSO office which was just five minutes away on Thống Nhứt Boulevard. Here again was the big difference between East and West. It took me a few minutes of easy driving to the ESSO garage in front of my office. In NYC, every workday, I had to take a rapid, noisy and crowded subway from uptown Columbia university campus station to Canal street station in lower Manhattan near Wall Street. But now I missed the traditional reading of the New York Times held with only one hand and standing in a crowded subway during the commute.

At 27, my greatest challenge was to lay down a sound road map for my future; I wanted a stable job, a comfortable home within my means, and last but not least, a companion for life. I decided to settle down permanently in Saigon. In the West, after the completion of my training, life was comfortable but I missed my parents and my extended family. I did not forget that my most important objective in life was to be trained as a good engineer to go home and serve my underdeveloped motherland.

My first job was already secured even before leaving New York City. Mr. George P. Case, the general manager of ESSO Vietnam, during his trip to White Plains New York, had offered me a job upon my return home. (See chapter 11. Inside Story ESSO.) With my savings at Esso, I found a nice two floor apartment near "Hồ Tắm Chi Lăng" or "Chi Lăng Swimming Pool" in Gia Định, a suburb of Saigon. My starter home was a fixer-upper. My pride and joy was the well-lit miniature pond with rocks, plants, waterfall, and goldfish that I had built in the dining room.

With my professional background, I had no problem solving my first two pre-requirements for marriage: job and home. Next, finding a wife, appeared to be the most difficult and complicated task of all. I had no coaching or experience in this matter. Of course, I had been raised with strong family values. My parents were married for more than 70 years, and that was in its own right a great example. I realized also that behind every successful man there was a good woman. How was I to solve this monumental challenge of finding the right partner?

I looked at the marriages of my sisters, brother, other family members and friends for guidance. Luckily, I was the youngest in the family and could learn from the experiences of my siblings. They had all followed the traditional system of Confucian family values, and went forward with the marriages that their parents had pre-arranged. Traditionally, all of the in-laws belonged to the same social class. Fortunately, five out of the five sisters enjoyed successful, happy marriages. My brother Five was the exception, as his marriage ended in divorce. His second marriage was of his own choosing. Additionally, each of my six uncles was also married just once in their lives.

It is common knowledge that the success of any man's life has a lot to do with the personality of his wife. I just wanted to have a normal, simple, and modest life from beginning to end. I had a lot to learn from my brother who had unconditionally accepted a pre-arranged marriage. He was just a student in high school and was called home to become manager of the family rice mill. Shortly thereafter, he got married to the young woman that had been chosen by the family. Although this arrangement worked well for my sisters, it failed miserably in my brother's case. The incompatibility of their personalities became apparent, and their union was unsustainable.

In Vietnam, we have this saying "Dò Sông Dò Biển Dễ Dò, Nào Ai Có Thước Để Đo Lòng Người," meaning "To measure a river or an ocean is easy, but there is no yardstick to measure the human soul." The wisdom I gained from this saying gave me the courage to tell my parents that I would choose my own wife. It was a normal western concept that proved alien to my own eastern tradition. I would welcome my parents' introduction to the daughters of their friends but the final decision should be mine. I was pleased and relieved that they agreed with my wish. Frankly, they seemed to realize that they would not choose better than I. In addition, they recognized that I had been influenced by the American way of life after many years of living independently and successfully in the United States.

I knew that choosing the right woman to be my partner would be of utmost importance, as it would impact the rest of my life. I was fortunate to have a certain degree of notoriety from the popular monthly magazine, "Gia-Đình" or "Family," shown above. It implicitly announced that I was still an eligible bachelor. I hoped that this publicity would help me meet many attractive marriage prospects.

Of course, my friends and family were all eager to help. Over the next eighteen months, while I worked in Saigon, my mother introduced me to the daughter of one of her good friends. My father himself introduced me to the daughter of his close friend and neighbor. My co-worker at Esso, Hoàng Chấn fixed a date for me with his cousin. I contacted the younger sister of my buddy and classmate Robert Vĩnh Mậu from

Lycée Yersin; a Vietnamese friend of mine, Phó Bá Long, who had attended Harvard while I was at MIT, arranged a meeting for me with his younger sister… So far, no one struck me as just the right partner… In Vietnam people often say that "marriage is either like playing the lottery, or it is pre-destination." It's either an act of God, or just plain luck. I remember wishing that this process of choosing a wife came with a practical check list for the neophyte!

One day, a close cousin of mine, Khương Hữu Thị Hiệp, living next door, told me that her husband Dr. Hồ Trung Dung's family was preparing a father's Memorial Day reunion. By tradition, many relatives would get together on that day for a feast. It was the time for the family gourmet chefs to show off their special recipes. She invited me to join her so she could introduce me to the daughter of her in-law's relatives. Of course, I willfully and thankfully accepted the offer. We were together at the home of Mr. and Mrs. Phan Kiến Khương, President of the Vietnam Bar. It was on this occasion that I first saw Marie. I liked Marie right off the bat. My cousin had known her for many years, and knew that she came from a good family, so no background check was necessary. She was just 21, and still a pharmacy student at Saigon University.

Marie and mother

Marie as a student in pharmacy

Marie's father was an engineer who had gone to the famous École Centrale de Paris, the "MIT" of France. Marie's grandfather was the first minister of Public Works of Vietnam. As an engineer, I was pleased to be able to converse with her relatives on the same level.

Marie's grandparents surrounded by children and grandchildren
2nd from far right: Marie; 1st from far left: Marie's mother

I found Marie to be a natural, calm beauty. She wore no make-up, flashy jewelry, high heels, or loud clothing. She projected a low-key personality, and preferred privacy. On the flip side, I was driven and highly competitive, having struggled for both grades and my survival - alone in a foreign country for many years. I thought that Marie's quiet personality would be compatible with mine. She could help me, a type A, to be calmer and in doing so, lead me to a less stressful life. That was more than I could ask for. I was convinced that the long search for the right wife was over. I wanted to marry Marie.

With my good job at Esso, I had financial independence, so Marie would not need to open a pharmacy to bring in a second income. I felt very fortunate that Marie came from an honest family, as I really appreciated that quality in life, particularly in my later career. Among all the candidates, Marie offered me the most appeal on every level - physically, morally and spiritually. God had presented me with a companion for life, who was beautiful both inside and out.

Everything seemed to be going well so far, but I still had one big obstacle to face. By tradition, my family was Confucian and Buddhist, but Marie's family came from three generations of fervent Catholics. The Catholic Church in Vietnam was very strict about inter-faith marriage. According to the catholic doctrine, I needed to convert to Catholicism before I could be married in the Catholic Church, and also agree that any future children would be raised Catholic. No exceptions or Marie would be excommunicated. I found all of this a little arbitrary and rather unfair, but God did give me a break. In the U.S. I had taken a course in world religions during my sophomore year and I was convinced that most religions were good.

Since Marie's father had studied in Paris for many years, he had been exposed to Western culture and its liberal thinking. I asked for an appointment to see him in his office to present my point of view about religion. As I had anticipated, he appeared to be very open-minded. He listened to my opinion and spoke fairly softly. Firstly, I pointed out that Christianity, (both Catholic and Protestant), along with Buddhism, Hinduism, Judaism, and others were all good religions. And if, just for the purpose of having my wedding, I were to play the game and say to the priest that I wanted to drop Buddhism in order to get his blessing, then after the ceremony I would still remain the same person. Now that would be sheer hypocrisy!

I also pointed out that from the day children were born, they did not know anything about religion, so how could they choose Catholicism? I felt that at 18, as an adult, my own children should be able to freely adopt any religion of their choice. Marie's father seemed to accept my explanation but the priest would not. I thought the Catholic Church was too narrow minded or even cruel to excommunicate Marie because of my own decision to marry her. With this impasse, I decided that we would get married not in the church, but in the office of the mayor of my district.

Fortunately, a few years later, with more liberalization in the Vietnamese Catholic community, the priest at "Dòng Chúa Cứu Thế," the Redemptorist Church near my home on Kỳ Đồng Street agreed to officiate at a church wedding if I agreed to let the children be Catholic. I did not have to be Catholic, just the children! This way Marie would not be excommunicated.

According to tradition, we had an engagement celebration at Marie's home. Dinner was prepared by a well-known catering service in Saigon for a large extended family get-together.

Engagement dinner at the front yard of Marie's home

Marie and my niece Thu at the engagement dinner, 1960

About six months later, on November 22, 1960, Marie and I were officially married in the mayor's office near our home. The family ceremony was held at the villa at 83 Ngô Thời Nhiệm Street.

Wedding Day, November 22, 1960 at home 83 Ngô Thời Nhiệm St

Typically, we had a celebration dinner organized at the well-known Ngọc Lan Đình restaurant in Cholon for members of the extended family and guests. Altogether twenty tables with twelve guests each. By tradition, near the end of the dinner, both bride, groom and their parents walked from table to table to thank the guests but also to receive their best wishes and their money envelopes.

My father and uncles by the ancestral altar

The next day, we traveled with our VW beetle to Dalat, the Pearl of the Highlands, for our honeymoon at the famous Lang Bian Palace hotel. The war was on and some fighting caused interruptions to our trip. The Viet Cong had just blown up a bridge on the road to Dalat. One of my friends, Mr. Hannon from CARIC, a French construction company in Saigon, used his company's ferry boat to carry my VW across the Saigon River to a detour route on the other side of the city.

Marie and I settled into family life at our new home in Gia Định. My previous experience in dealing with hardships and challenges were of great help to me; however, Marie came from a very sheltered background with very few real-life experiences. My mother found a full time cook to assist Marie. "Dì Chín," my Aunt Nine, came from my mother's extended family in the Mekong Delta. She knew Vietnamese bourgeois cooking, and in exchange had room and board in our new home. Gradually, Marie learned to cook.

My three years working at ESSO were enjoyable and I was sent to attend management training seminars in Hong Kong and Singapore. I was responsible for the good management of service stations throughout South Vietnam. The company reserved for me a black four-door Chevrolet for my inspection trips. For the first time in my life, I knew my country from the southernmost town of Cà Mau to the northernmost city of Quảng Trị. The country had beautiful white sand beaches at Vũng Tàu, Mũi Né, Cam Ranh, Nha Trang, Đại Lãnh (Cap Varella). But the most scenic site was the ESSO terminal at Liên Chiểu near the "Hải Vân" or "Sea-Cloud" Pass. I had a very good souvenir of that spectacular place run by my buddy engineer Huỳnh Ngọc Châu.

Life as a manager in ESSO was comfortable and all right but my main objective in life was to develop my country not a foreign company. For three years I learned a lot about the fundamentals of business management in a multinational corporation and it was about time for me to prepare for my take-off. In 1961, the war in Vietnam became hotter and the government gave draft deferment only to managers of state corporations. I was lucky to be the right man, at the right time and at the right place.

The Vietnam Sugar Company had a multi-million dollar modernization project at the important Hiệp Hoà mill, near the Cambodian border. I got the new job as technical director and managed that project. I did not realize that the Viet Cong (VC) in that infested area wanted to sabotage the company to paralyze the economy. In fact, I almost lost my life twice while working there. Chapter 12, "Perils of Industrialization during War Time" will go into the details.

Marie and I led a frugal life from the early years. In 1962, with our savings and the assistance of my father, we moved into a bigger home with a front yard garden at

11 Kỳ Đồng Street, Saigon. The war activities became more intense. It was not safe to drive to the country side for weekend relaxation. I began to think about the design of a front yard and a roof garden to enjoy nature in the security of the city. The façade of the house was thickly covered by tropical evergreens obstructing the direct view from the street and the solar glare. From the ground floor, one could see the front of the third floor roof garden with "bamboo curtain" 5 meter high avoiding vis-à-vis of surrounding home windows. (see photo below)

Façade: 2nd & 3rd floor with roof garden, a 5 meter high bamboo curtain avoiding vis a vis windows. Green leaves façade avoiding direct view from street, 1965

Third floor roof garden with fruit trees, herbs, bonsai, bar and pool, 1965

Having an integrated roof garden was a novel idea in 1963 in Saigon. By integrated garden I meant the concrete flat roof covered with grass. There would be a small pool, herb garden, and aquatic plants with gold fish. At the garden corners, yard high planters provided soil for fruit trees like papaya and Longan. I planted winter melon, Obo, a bitter melon with their beautiful gourds hanging from a horizontal frame.

Singapore garden at every floor

Another recent roof and wall garden in Paris

In front of the house, I designed an Asian garden with a pond the shape of Vietnam divided in two by the 17th parallel Bến Hải Bridge according to the 1954 Geneva Convention.

My father and I went to the Mekong Delta to look for a rare and beautiful "Mai" Luck blossom bonsai for the center piece. (See photos) The beauty of this plant was

My home was also the place where I could entertain international teams visiting Vietnam to help in the implementation of development projects. My team cooperated continuously with the USAID economic team. To improve our working conditions and our public relations, I often organized dinner parties at my home so that the two teams could have the opportunity to do some shop talk in a friendly atmosphere. A typical PR dinner started with guests on the roof garden for the aperitif served by the well-known Caravelle hotel catering team wearing white gloves. After that, guests walked down to the ground floor dining room with four round tables of ten each. At the end of the stairs, each guest checked the seating charts consisting of four circles of names for the seating arrangement. (See photos)

Guests going down to dining room from roof garden

Dinner for IDB & USAID team members on the ground floor
On my left: Mr. von Spiegelfeld #3 USAID; in front, Mr. Bennett #2 USAID

When I was working for the Hiệp Hoà sugar mill project, I needed the help of an expert in electrical engineering. Fortunately, I found Mr. Hồ Tấn Phát, CEO of Vietnam Power Company. We became close friends in 1962. His company's home with tennis court and swimming pool became the meeting place of our little social club. Regularly, every Wednesday from noon to 2 PM [normal 2 hours lunch break system] and on weekends, we played doubles tennis there. Our other partners were the late Mr. Nguyễn văn Bông, head of the National Institute of Administration and Mr. Trần quí Thân, head of Đông Phương (Orient) bank.

The year 1964 was an important milestone in my new life in Saigon. Happily married, I settled down in a cozy home and enjoyed life with an interesting job and a circle of good friends. I was eager and ready to tackle any new challenge in my career. By luck and pure coincidence, Bửu Hoan, the director of the Industrial Development Center (IDC), a government agency in Saigon, got a new job representing Vietnam at the World Bank in Washington D.C. I was the right man at the right time to get his job under the sponsorship of the ministry of economy. With my experience of advanced management at Esso and as technical director of a big industrial corporation, I was ready to meet the challenge of developing the industry of the country especially under wartime conditions. Right away, I was thinking of forming a strong team of technocrats to face the new tough task. Being the first Vietnamese MIT engineer returning to Vietnam from a New York job, I worked with the American University Alumni Association (AUAA) to recruit my new staff. I started immediately the training trainers program to speed up the agency's technical strength. I contacted the Phú Thọ National Engineering School to hire their graduates. I convinced the Board of Directors to approve a competitive salary scale to avoid corruption and to motivate the work force. Every Tuesday morning at 7:30AM exactly, 40 executive members of our team got together in the conference room. Those who came late were locked out of the meeting room. This little discipline seemed to be useful. Each member was assigned an industrial project, one month in advance, for research work and future presentation in this room. The assignments also demanded some public speaking know-how. Following the presentations, the speaker had to answer the questions from the audience. Near the end of the meeting, it was my turn to summarize the strong and weak points of the project including the quality of the presentation. Years later, during our San Francisco reunion, everybody told me that they had butterflies in the stomach on that unforgettable day.

It was also a known fact that a CEO of any government financial institution was subject to political nomination and thus provided the parties an opportunity to collect campaign funds. I wanted to avoid the usual metaphorical "musical chairs" each time a new government was formed. That was easier said than done. One of my career achievements was to be able to hold the same good job from 1964 to 1975 i.e. to the last days of Saigon. How to survive the political pressure for eleven years? I prayed God to give me the lucidity of mind and the courage to express clearly and correctly what I had seen and learned in Vietnam. I used a lot of common sense and strict discipline against temptation. Corruption is everywhere in the world. In underdeveloped countries, it's cash and/or gold. In the U.S. it is the lobby by thousands of lawyers in Washington DC.

I made sure that I and my staff remained honest thanks to our decent and fair salaries. All should do their best in their jobs and face constant strong competition from the outside. The annual auditing with the participation of USAID (United States Agency for International Development) was very severe. There existed one very serious loophole! What would happen if I were honest but my wife silently, secretly and intelligently played with money under the table? In most cases of this common oriental practice only God knew. The Vietnamese kept saying: "It's easy to measure rivers and oceans but there is no yardstick to measure the human mind." During my decade of working in the finance sector, I had to face and combat the pressure and temptation of corruption. It was no surprise when friends and relatives of high government officials often approached me to ask for favors. I simply said that if the investment project met the check list of the bank, then it would be processed very rapidly. One time, I received a phone call from the Prime Minister's wife dealing with the financing of a textile plant and my answer was the same as in other cases. On another occasion, I was surprised to see General Loan, former head of the national police, walking with a cane into my office. After a brief conversation, he said he wanted a loan to open a jewelry shop. I told him politely that a jewelry shop was not on my industrial project list. That was the end of the story. Another time General Tôn Thất Đính applied for a loan for a printing plant under another name. He got the loan because his project met the bank requirements. However, later on, I had delays with its payment schedule and I started to have problems with him; but then it was April 1975!

During the Moon Cake season, in my office, I got a phone call from my wife Marie. At home, she received a gift bag full of Moon cakes with cash underneath. Marie had no problem returning the bag immediately then called to let me know about it. Marie told me that the reasons for people to bring us gifts varied. One man said that, thanks to the bank loan, he became very rich and this was his way of saying thanks. He insisted that it was not a bribe. Of course, Marie let me know immediately and had put a stop to all of those cases. One more entertaining case: because we had no children, one man tried to persuade us to accept his gift of precious jade and gold with the explanation that they would bring us a son! The greatest gift that God has given me is an honest wife and after more than half a century living together I think God has helped me in my successful career.

Besides being honest, I had to work hard with my team of "Young Turks" to show real performance. I noted that, to avoid defaults in the repayment of industrial loans, investors needed competent managers to maintain high productivity at their plants. I established the Management Association of Vietnam to offer training seminars on a regular basis.

Victor Hugo said "ceux qui vivent ce sont ceux qui luttent." i.e. "those who live are those who fight." I succeeded to forestall the competition from political appointees because I was ready to fight for my good cause. Allow me to use the "boxing ring metaphor." If I kept performing well in a boxing ring, it would be difficult for me to be knocked down by any political appointee. Moreover, smart competitors should look for easier boxing matches. Why take risk and maybe go to fifteen bloody rounds and not be certain of the result. Thank God, I did not have to go to the ring with anyone in the eleven years of work. My most rewarding souvenir of the whole career in Vietnam was the complete surprise party on my 70th birthday in the US, organized silently on the internet by the Saigon "Young Turks" team. Although they were dispersed all over the world after April 1975, they gathered together in 2000 at my modest home in San Francisco to celebrate the most moving and meaningful reunion of my career! (See photo next page)

My Saigon Life from 1958-1975

Hàng 1: Chị VHùng, Chị LTMưu, Chị LHồ, Thảo, Chị KHDiệu, Anh KHDiệu, Chị PMTâm, Chị NĐCường, Chị Mộng Hoàng, Chị LTTạo
Hàng 2: VThức, Chị VThức, HĐNhã, Chị NĐKhôi, Chị TVKhởi, Chị NĐChiến, Chị TCNghĩa, Anh TCNghĩa, VHùng, LHồ, PMTâm, NĐChiến
Hàng 3: NNĐiền, NĐKhôi, NĐCường, TVKhởi, LTMưu, NKDõ, NVChâu, HHHân, BTQNhơn, LTTạo, NVHùng

Oct. 2000. Photo taken in my backyard. An absolute surprise party on my 70th birthday. Many team members not been seen since April 15, 1975

It was one of the most joyful moments in my life. They all have new successful careers in the New World holding executive positions in corporate America such as PacBell, Pennzoil, Esso, Halliburton, PG&E etc…

Fate and Destiny

Looking back at my 17 years of life in Saigon from 1958 to 1975, I must say that it was filled with numerous mixed feelings about that very crucial time of my life as well as that of the Vietnamese people. On the one hand, I was so happy in 1958 to be back with my family after the long stay in the U. S. for my professional training, to visit again the enjoyable Mekong Delta of my teenage years, to have a good job at Esso, Vietnam Sugar Company and the IDB. I was able to marry a wonderful wife while respecting the Vietnamese Confucian traditions but also exercising at the same time the freedom of the American way of life to marry the person of my own choice and not one dictated by my parents. Then there was my long involvement in the South Vietnamese government with lots of sweat and tears to overcome enormous challenges. With my professional skills acquired in the U. S., I was able to give the best of myself for the industrial development of South Vietnam.

At least I can say to myself that during my 14 years of service in the South Vietnamese government, I made concrete and substantial contributions to my underdeveloped Vietnam, a country in a difficult war time condition. I almost lost my life twice during my field trips to the project worksites. The combination of my knowledge of modern western technology and my traditional Confucian values were again successful in blending themselves together in this "East meets West" happening and made me a better-rounded technician for serving my country.

On the other hand, I also had to live through the dramatic episode of the war leading to the fall of Saigon by the invading North Vietnamese troops on April 30, 1975 and the loss of freedom by the imposition of communist rule on the entire country.

Do I have any regrets during my years in Saigon? Yes, in a number of aspects, most of all about the failure to save South Vietnam from communist rule in spite of all our efforts.

The main objective of the Vietnamese nationalists during three decades of the prolonged deadly conflict against Ho Chi Minh and his communist rule in North Vietnam was to defend and preserve freedom and democracy for the Vietnamese people. After the 1954 Geneva Conference, it became the limited objective of maintaining a non-communist South Vietnam with the vital American economic and military assistance.

However, it was also the continued policy of all the American administrations involved in the Vietnamese conflict from Eisenhower to Nixon that the enemy, North Vietnam, would not be invaded and occupied by American and/or South Vietnamese ground forces. In other words, the American government did not advocate the complete destruction of the enemy by a military victory in the conventional sense of warfare. Clearly, the U. S. took this position to avoid having the Vietnam war turned into a global hot war between the U. S. and the entire communist bloc including the Soviet Union and Communist China. This U. S. strategic position was no effective deterrent against North Vietnam's permanent threat to invade South Vietnam by the NVA forces which had already demonstrated their capability with their resounding victory over the French troops at Điện Biên Phủ in 1954.

It was surely because of this constant threat of massive invasion of South Vietnam by the entire North Vietnamese Army (NVA) that the Saigon brass were able to take power in the Saigon government after the overthrow and murder of President Ngô Đình Diệm on November 2nd 1963 (which was followed 20 days later by the assasination of the U. S. President John F. Kennedy). Then there was no doubt in the mind of President Lyndon Baines Johnson that North Vietnam was quite capable of carrying out an all out invasion of South Vietnam after the Saigon military coup in 1963. By that time there were only about 23,000 non-combat "American advisers" who had arrived during the presidency of John F. Kennedy. The only way for the U. S. to prevent such an invasion by the NVA was the introduction of American combat troops into South Vietnam which began in March 1965 with the landing. on the beaches of Da Nang, of two Marine battalions that were welcomed with flowers by joyful Vietnamese schoolgirls in their traditional white tunics. By the end of that year 1965, the number of U. S. combatants rapidly climbed to over 180,000, then to nearly 400,000 in the following year 1966, then again to over 480,000 in 1967. Eventually, that number peaked at over half a million GIs by 1968!

George Clemenceau said "War is too important to be left to the generals." In the case of South Vietnam, generals not only monopolized the war, they left no power to the civilian executives! The civil administration of the country was dominated by the armed forces. The graduates of the National Institute of Administration were under the supervision of the lesser qualified military officers. Among the elite of South Vietnam, most generals were the least educated.

With the war raging on more fiercely everyday from 1960 in the aftermath of the decision of the Politburo in Hanoi to create the so-called NLF and to "liberate" South Viet Nam by both military and political means, even President Ngô Đình Diệm began to see the necessity to appoint army officers to be provincial governors in order to deal with the worsening security situation. The people in South Vietnam soon saw that not only were the provincial governors army officers but so were the district chiefs

- not to mention that from 1965 at the very top the president and the prime minister were army generals as well!

A funny example of this sad situation was the farcical case of the nomination, as minister of culture, of "D M", the last of the least qualified generals in cultural matters. For many long years this general was a well known army colonel responsible for "military security and intelligence" without much involvement in cultural affairs. He was given the cabinet minister ranking in the civilian government following the 1963 coup d'état probably for having given his support to the Buddhist activists in their revolt against the Ngô Đình Diệm government. Anyway, he only lasted a few months at that cabinet post. As the saying goes "That's the way the cookie crumbles."

Like many people I also have regrets and sadness about the way the U. S. ended its intervention in the Vietnam conflict. One may say the original sin was, after WWII, when President Truman helped and financed France to reoccupy Indochina, its former colony. Then, President Eisenhower did try to convince the French government to prevent a takeover of power by Ho Chi Minh and his communist group but also to give back independence to the Vietnamese people. France did not go along with this American advice and the French mission was ended by its defeat at Điện Biên Phủ in 1954 along with the abilition of French Indochina. Next, after the Geneva Conference of 1954, everybody could see that the increasing economic and military assistance given by the U. S. was to help South Vietnam contain Red China and the spread of communism in Southeast Asia, the "Domino Theory" as coined by President Eisenhower!"

The people in South Vietnam were constantly reminded of the formidable American presence by the endless humming of helicopters in the sky. To this end, there was also the enormous American military base in Cam Ranh Bay which made a big impression. The United States Naval Mobile Construction Battalion (CB), the Seabees, built the huge Cam Ranh Bay staging area with an airfield designed for B-52s and Boeing 747s. This U. S. Cam Ranh naval base not only provided firepower to the military operations in both South and North Viet Nam but it was also the largest U. S. naval base in the Pacific Ocean theater. Like many people, I thought that this Cam Ranh base was only not designed for guerilla warfare but meant to stay there for a long time like many other U. S. naval bases in the world. This U. S. Cam Ranh base did give me and many other South Vietnamese a sense of assurance of continued American assistance. However, after President Nixon and Secretary Kissinger sipped tea with Mao Tse Tung and Zhou Enlai in Beijing in February 1972, the North Vietnamese knew that the end of the U. S. intervention in South Vietnam was near. This came quite quickly, less than a year later, with the signing of the Paris Agreement in January 1973, thanks to the efforts of Lê Đức Thọ and Henry Kissinger, both receiving the 1973 Nobel Peace Prize for that fete. Nevertheless, through the cessation of its military intervention in the Vietnam war, the total withdrawal and the return of the U. S. POWs, the U. S. did reserve a surprise for Chairman Mao and Premier Zhou because in April 1975, South Vietnam was handed to North Vietnam, in other words, given to the communist Soviets and not to the communist Chinese! That, of course, did not help improve the relations between Viet Nam and China. In February 1979, Beijing had to give Ha Noi a quick military slap as a lesson in keeping good manners between neighbors. The same story of good or bad neighbors between Vietnam and China is still going on ... Is the U. S. now returning to help the Vietnamese deal with their traditional big and somewhat oppressive neighbor? Forty years ago, America, the Number One Superpower, did abandon South Vietnam when the ARVN was left without any ammo and petroleum to fight the all out invasion by 20 divisions of the North Vietnamese Army NVA ... That was the decisive time and a fateful event I and all other Vietnamese nationalists must live to remember.

After reading the draft of my book, the Pulitzer Award reporter Peter Arnett said: "It was you and your childhood friends who helped create the South Vietnam that America *initially supported and then abandoned.*"

My wife and I lost everything and were lucky to survive as refugees in Marine Camp Pendleton, Ca. It marked a fresh start of my second life in the New World. (See Photo from the Associated Press below, taken on my arrival at Camp Pendleton).

An End... and New Beginnings

Khung Huu Dieu, ex-banker, shows his wealth—clothes for family.

Khương Hữu Điểu, ex-banker, shows his wealth---clothes for family

PART V

A Nation Governed in Time of War

CHAPTER 11

ESSO – The Inside Story

Where you get all the extras!

Gas station in Saigon

Upon starting my job at Esso in Saigon, it did not take me long to notice that the Mr. Case I worked with in Saigon was completely different from the man I had met in New York. He was, indeed, a real Dr. Jekyll and Mr. Hyde. In fact, his leadership style was that of an imperialist colonial administrator, carried over from the British Empire days in India where he had worked for the ESSO Company.

Thống Nhứt Blvd with Saigon Cathedral on the left and the ESSO building on the right

During my seven-year stay in the US, a dramatic event happened to my country: at the Geneva Conference in 1955, Vietnam was partitioned at the 17th parallel into a communist North Vietnam and a non-communist South Vietnam which rapidly ceased to exist as the State of Vietnam under Emperor Bảo Đại and became the Republic of Vietnam under President Ngô Đình Diệm. This new Republic of Vietnam received much aid from America, thanks to the US Secretary of State John Foster Dulles who was a staunch anti-communist.

When I returned to Saigon in 1958 to join the ESSO company, I still had the impression of coming back to my country Vietnam but did not fully realize that it was no longer the Vietnam I had left in 1952. It was only half of what used to be my homeland and country! The many changes and differences which had taken place during my stay in the US began to manifest themselves gradually to me when I assumed my job at ESSO

It must be said that by the end of the 1950s there was already a large presence of Americans in Saigon and South Vietnam. Most of them were there as "advisers" without any formal authorization for combat action as of yet although President Kennedy did quietly say the US troops could act in self-defense when being attacked. A lot of that would come a few years later!

Mention must be made here that ESSO, SHELL and CALTEX were the only three oil companies supplying all the petroleum products to the South Vietnamese Armed Forces and government organizations as well as the American Embassy and other US agencies operating in South Vietnam. These were huge contracts which were carried out constantly under pressing urgency and high security conditions.

In the task of receiving and delivering petroleum products, my American training was more than sufficient for me to deal with the scientific and technological problems encountered by ESSO. In terms of working relationships, the atmosphere I found there was not the best to be expected but that was not a great surprise to me. After nearly one hundred years of French colonial rule, a condescending attitude towards the local population was expected from foreigners with some authority. For those of us who had acquired higher education and professional qualifications in France or the United States, as was in my case with MIT, we were treated slightly better than the typical Vietnamese subordinates.

Not all the expatriates at Esso were of high caliber. Many of them were probably at the high school level in their countries but they were sent to Saigon to do some specific jobs for which they had the necessary skills and experience. That was the case with Bob Bell, the Australian redneck, who was the terminal manager at my first job at the Nhà Bè terminal in the suburb of Saigon. Tankers from Indonesia went up the Saigon River to deliver their loads of petroleum products to the Nhà Bè tank farms. It was the distribution hub of ESSO products to the entire country.

ESSO tanker at Nhà Bè, Saigon River

Bob Bell used foul language with frequent fits of anger at work. I was repulsed by everything about him - the way he wore his Australian style cowboy hat, the way he spoke with white foam coming out on the sides of his mouth, and the way he walked with a swing like a tough master sergeant in front of a group of neophyte soldiers. He bragged about his buddy-buddy social life at his sumptuous residence inside the Terminal with the American big boss by the name of Mitchell, the powerful operations manager at the head office, in order to impose his authority at the Nhà Bè Terminal.

At the terminal, I was given a French style villa next door to my friend, Nguyễn Ngọc Châu, a Vietnamese engineer who had been educated in France. The original red roof tiles of the villa I was supposed to live in, however, had been replaced by rusty sheets of galvanized iron, so I told Bob Bell that it looked like a chicken house, and I refused to live in it. Fortunately, he did not like my attitude, and soon I was sent back at Saigon to work at the ESSO main office. That had been my intention. There was no life for me in that no man's land of a tank farm. What a contrast it was from my previous job on Broadway in New York City!

At the Saigon office, I was placed under the supervision of an old French navy engineer, Mr. Henry. He probably felt threatened by my credentials, so after my first month at ESSO, he came to my office one day and asked me to take an exam!

I reacted fairly fast. I closed the office door and said "OK, Mr. Henry, you write ten questions and I'll write ten questions. We'll put the questions in the hat, and then pull out the questions and take the exam together." The whole time I was telling myself that I'd worked in New York City doing more advanced engineering tasks than this, and nobody challenged my knowledge, and yet here in this little under-developed country, I was getting this kind of treatment. I said to myself "Besides, I am still full of engineering knowledge, so how can this guy outsmart me?" I was standing against the door not letting him get out. He was really locked in. After a short silence, he cracked a smile. He was joking, he said. There would be no test, and no exam. Oh boy, he made my day! My sweat at MIT had paid off.

In spite of my rocky start, I had a pleasant life during my time with ESSO. Being away from Vietnam for seven years, I was anxious to familiarize myself with my new half of the country from south to north up to the 17th parallel, and my job with ESSO gave me the opportunity to travel. ESSO gas stations were built all over South Vietnam and making inspection tours of all those stations became part of my responsibility. I would stop at every ESSO station, take photos, and make suggestions on how to improve its management.

Village "station" with a gas drum and a hand pump, ESSO sign full of bullet holes

Small hand pump station   *Old Gilbarco pump*

Vintage gas pump

Typical station in the province

The company gave me a big, black, four-door Chevrolet and a chauffeur in white uniform and I was on my own. The biggest problem I found was that many stations were cheating on the volume of gasoline sold to the customers. According to an old design, each pump had two 5 liter glass cylinders as a measuring device. To cheat, the station manager would break the lead control seal at the pump, and put glass balls into the glass cylinders. The lead control seal was then carefully repaired and replaced. As a result, the customers would end up paying for more gasoline than they actually received. At the end of my inspection tour, I had collected a big basketful of those glass balls. My job was to catch all the cheaters at the gas stations. The solution was to convince the dealers that they would lose their gas stations if they got caught in the future. Besides, I designed a better control lead seal for the pumps. Cheaters would be prosecuted severely by the local authority.

I had numerous opportunities to visit the Mekong Delta in the late 1950s and I gained a good appreciation of the life of the simple people in the rural areas in contrast to the richer city dwellers. The general security situation then was still quite good. I could travel by car day or night all over South Vietnam. There were, of course, occasional terrorist activities and assassinations by the Viet Cong. Now and then, they would target village and district chiefs, teachers and social workers, doctors and government officials, or blow up market places and theaters, but there was not a real war yet. It was only by 1959 that the communist Politburo in Hanoi officially declared that the "political struggle to liberate South Vietnam" must become a "military-political struggle" and, by Decision 559 of the North Vietnamese Defense Ministry, the so-called Ho Chi Minh Trail for the north-south infiltration of armaments and hundreds of thousands of North Vietnamese troops was set up. This was quickly followed by Decision 759 which established the infiltration routes by sea.

It was by the end of 1960 that Hanoi created the so-called "National Liberation Front" (NLF) to masquerade the North Vietnamese military aggression as a "popular uprising" in the South to fight the "American imperialists and their puppets" to liberate South Vietnam. Then the intensity of the Vietnam conflict began to escalate with the increasing attacks in South Vietnam by the regular units of the North Vietnamese (NVA). But life in Saigon and the large cities was normal and peaceful. I was not worried by the idea of a very hypothetical military victory by the Hanoi troops against the Saigon forces who were receiving the tremendous economic and military aid from the American government, the Number One Superpower and Leader of the Free World!

Therefore, at the time I was regularly touring the country for ESSO. I was delighted to rediscover the many places of my pleasant childhood years. The Mekong Delta was a nice place to live in, a completely flat terrain with countless small rivers providing cheap and easy transportation routes and good irrigation for the vast paddy fields. Life was rather easy going for the rural population with ample harvests of paddy rice. Food was not scarce. There was plenty of fish and shrimp, and frogs - a popular delicacy, and lots of poultry, pork and more. That was very true in my native province of Định Tường. It was always with great joy when I returned to my hometown of Mỹ Tho to see my parents, siblings, relatives and childhood friends. Even after many long years in the US, I did not forget the delicious local dishes such the "lẩu lươn" eel soup, the exceptionally good crab of Bình Đại or the large crispy deep-fried fish seldom found elsewhere in the region. My hometown has always been famous all over the world with its "Hủ Tiếu Mỹ Tho", the rich and tasty Mỹ Tho noodle soup.

Hủ Tiếu Mỹ Tho

Nem

Well known also is the kind of Vietnamese fermented raw pork sausage called Nem Cai-Lậy. The meat is sweet, sour, salty and spicy.

Fresh nem rolls

My frequent trips for Esso allowed me to see that life was much more difficult in the central areas of South Vietnam with less arable land and harsher weather. Along the coast in Phan Thiết-Nha Trang region, there were huge salt flats that were utilized for the production of anchovy sauce. This area was the center for making Nước Mắm (fish sauce) in Vietnam. Further north I saw immense tea and coffee plantations. My trips also took me to the highlands along the Lao and Cambodian borders, mainly with thick jungles and mountains, where life had been difficult for centuries, especially for the nomadic ethnic minorities in the jungles.

During French colonial rule, tea and rubber plantations were established in the highlands by the French colonialists with the local Vietnamese labor. I visited many of the French rubber plantations because they required lots of petroleum products for their operations. On the large rubber plantations for Michelin and other large companies, latex was gathered and sent back to France for the making of tires. The French bosses at these opulent and deluxe plantations continued to live in beautiful old colonial mansions with plenty of cheap servants to wait on them like royalty, and gourmet chefs to cook for them. They enjoyed Olympic size swimming pools with crystal pure water, and clean air away from the city pollution. They would travel back and forth to Saigon in their little private planes. During this time period, I earned a comfortable salary and had the unique opportunity to see every part of Vietnam for the first time in my life. I had this wonderful chance to truly get to know my country. For the long term however, this life was not acceptable to me, as a professional engineer from MIT. I felt that my role in this multinational company was to learn the sophisticated management techniques that would enable me to do bigger jobs in the future. I wanted to take advantage of the company's excellent management sessions given by Louis Allen himself in Singapore and Hong Kong to further my professional foundation, and I was given the chance to do so!

In 1960 in Singapore, I finished a management-training program by Booz Allen Hamilton Inc., the world-famous consulting company. Upon my return to Saigon, I got, in my opinion, the best assignment in ESSO. I was appointed to the job of "Work Simplification Coordinator." I loved the job because it gave me the authorization to observe the existing operations of every department of the company. After observing each department, I made an analysis and a proposal for doing business more efficiently. For example, I made a flow chart tracking the complicated flow of paper through different offices in the company. Then, by streamlining the flow to the shortest path possible, it became evident where one could "trim the fat." By implementing the most efficient flow chart, management could accomplish the same results at lower costs. As a result, the company became more competitive. This kind of experience helped me a lot in my future work for the industrial development of my country.

In the meantime, my job at ESSO was so easy that after an eight-hour workday, I still had plenty of time to enjoy life with friends and family. Talking about the time of my years at ESSO, I cannot fail to mention the most important event of my whole existence: that was my marriage with Marie, my beloved wife who has shared with me every minute and second of all the ups and downs in the past 57 years and continues to be by my side now in our wonderful retirement in San Francisco.

I had a good job at ESSO and enjoyed my new home in Saigon with Marie but by 1961 the war in South Vietnam started to get worse with increased guerrilla activities by the Viet Cong together with more and more important military encounters between the North Vietnamese regular army units and the Saigon ARVN forces. The government then implemented a new policy of partial mobilization. People were drafted into the military from the private sector unless they were working for the government. So, I decided to leave ESSO and accepted the post of Technical Director for the Vietnam Sugar Company, a government joint venture with a group from France.

Little did I know then that I would remain continuously in the government service during the next 15 years and even reached positions at the cabinet levels in my early 30s with much sweat and tears waiting for me ahead. The ESSO years were probably the most enjoyable time of my life in Saigon and it was the sunshine before the beginning of the storm!

CHAPTER 12

Perils of Industrialization during War Time

Viet Cong found anywhere!

In 1961, the war in Vietnam became greatly intensified by communist North Vietnam after the public declaration by its leaders to "liberate South Vietnam by both military and political means." Security in the country side became a greater challenge to the government. After three years with ESSO, I had learned enough good management technique to last my career. However, there was no engineering challenge in the distribution of petroleum products from Saigon to the provinces. Work became dull for an engineer looking for a real challenging engineering job. In the meantime, the government tightened the mobilization program. Engineers like me were required to work for the government to obtain deferment. I decided to leave ESSO, a private sector, to accept the new job of Technical Director of the Vietnam Sugar Company, a government joint venture with a French group. This 90-year old Hiệp Hòa Sugarcane Joint Stock Company is one of the oldest and one of the best known sugar factories in Vietnam. The sugar mill site, about 50 Km from Saigon and only about 15 Km from the Cambodian border, was an area infested with communist insurgents. The Viet Cong (Viet Communists) had a safe haven on the Cambodian side of the river. At night, they often lobbed rockets onto the mill and/or the residential area of the staff. Daily, the personnel were exposed to kidnapping, assassination, mines on the access road and ambush of the supply convoy to the mill…The US Army named this place Cambodia's infamous "Parrot's Beak," a major Viet Cong (VC) staging area.

Red color area on the left: Cambodia

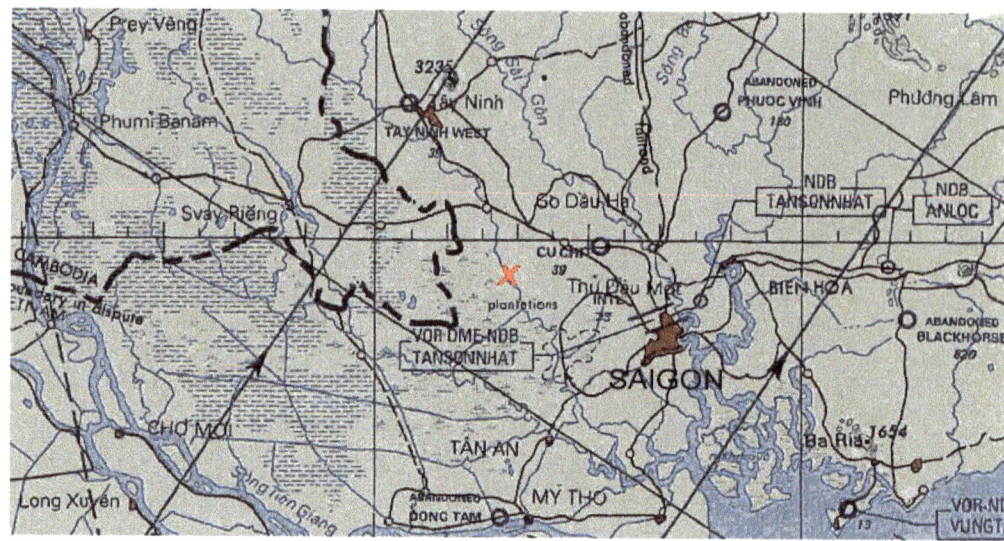
Area map: Red color cross showing Hiệp Hòa near Cambodian border in heavy black line

Hiệp Hòa Sugar Mill Modernization

As the new Technical Director, my first responsibility was to review the ongoing multi-million dollar modernization project of the Hiệp Hòa sugar mill. The order had been placed with the famous French company, SOCIÉTÉ Fives Lille Cail, Paris. To my great surprise, I found that the existing old steam reciprocating engine with a huge six-meter fly wheel was to be replaced by another similar steam reciprocating engine. Any modern design should use a steam turbine because it would be a much better machine from many engineering and financial points of view. In fact modern industry had already stopped installing those colossal reciprocating piston engines. For analogy, it's like a piston engine VS a jet engine. The team selecting the new mill equipment included an experienced senior French engineer, Mr. Polton from the famous École Polytechnique de Paris, and other Vietnamese engineers trained in Nantes and Lille, France. Mr. Polton was also Vice Chairman of the Board of Directors. Politically speaking, with Vietnam as a former French colony for almost a century, most of the executive leaders of Vietnam were trained in France. The technical adviser of Công Ty Đường Việt Nam was the Director General of the Planning Department, Mr. Huỳnh Văn Điễm, an engineer from the famous École Centrale de Paris.

After the defeat of Điện Biên Phủ in 1952, the French influence was gradually replaced by the American intervention. I happened to be the first engineer trained at MIT working with the existing team totally trained in France. Understandably there were some uneasy human relations. I was very careful in my presentation to the board about the unfortunate choice of the modernization equipment. The justification given to me was the steam from the existing boilers could not drive modern turbines. I had to face this semi-sophisticated technical challenge. Fortunately, at Ebasco in New York, I had worked with steam turbine projects and knew the subject quite well. I felt quite confident about my choice of modern turbine for the Hiệp Hòa Sugar Mill.

Mr. Polton then asked Fives Lille Cail to send an experienced engineer from Paris to discuss and work out the problem with me. I remembered inviting Mr. Pierre Mandois from Paris to do the engineering calculations for the turbine with me during the week-end at my home. Finally, Mr. Mandois agreed that the existing boilers were adequate to drive the turbines. As the next step, Mr. Mandois and I went together to Hiệp Hòa Sugar Mill to make sure that everything was OK for my solution before Mr. Mandois returned to Paris. We used an Air Vietnam Cessna plane for transport to avoid a VC road ambush during our trip to the mill.

We had to work late that day and stayed overnight at the site. We sent the plane back to Saigon. The mill staff sent a radio message to the Saigon head office for the Cessna the next day for our return. "Send BERLIET tomorrow to Hiệp Hòa." BERLIET is the name of a French truck company. I learned later that there were communist agents in the mill who understood the coded message.

Mr. Mandois and I boarded the plane at the mill airfield for Tân Sơn Nhứt Airport, Saigon. The Cessna took off smoothly but then at the end of the runway, the communists hidden in the tall sugar cane field hit it with a few dumdum bullets but missed the pilot and the passengers. I immediately looked at the fuel tank needle and saw it was still full. The pilot had some difficulty with the rudder and wing control cables. I saw him taking the plane up very fast to avoid additional bullets. God saved our lives because Saigon airport was a short distance by air from Hiệp Hòa airfield. With a light plane, even with engine trouble, we could glide for a long distance. Somehow, the pilot managed to make a rough landing and everybody survived the communist attack! Mr. Mandois returned to Paris to make sure that the new equipment could be manufactured on time to meet the critical schedule.

Another big surprise for me! The turbines were to be manufactured by the Fives Lille Cail Company but the castings of the huge flywheel of the steam engine was already done in France. The company sent a set of notarized shop photos to Hiệp Hòa management to prove their progress with the steam engine in other words Fives Lille wanted to continue with the existing contract. I had to go to the economic ministry committee to justify again my choice of the turbines. I repeated that the sugar company did choose the steam engine for the modernization project for two reasons: first the existing boilers could not run the turbines, second the Hiệp Hòa team could not handle modern turbines. Fives Lille Cail accepted my turbine solution but asked for compensation for the work done on the steam engine. I explained that at this time in

Vietnam we used tubeless tires. To play safe we could buy solid rubber tires to avoid flats but that was not modernization. My blunt explanation seemed to have worked.

My next problem was to make sure that the heavy concrete foundation for the turbines would meet the installation requirements. The communist objective was always to sabotage our mill to create a shortage of sugar and to provoke demonstrations by farmers against the government because of cane rotting in their fields due to the lack of grinding facilities. I was under tremendous pressure caused by VC infiltration around the mill site. The communists tried their best to disrupt the transport of the heavy equipment to the mill. I tried to do the opposite. The road from Saigon port to the mill had many bridges not capable of supporting heavy trucks. I decided to use a convoy of barges to transport the equipment to the mill via the Vàm Cỏ River.

War Time Logistics Problems

I had to learn my new lesson of how to work in war time Vietnam, how to ship equipment to the mill and avoid its sinking by the enemy.

Hiệp Hòa was located in HẬU NGHĨA Province next to Cambodia, the area in red at the top left corner of this map. It was so critical that the U.S. Navy had installed a Naval Advanced Tactical Support Base (ATSB) to defend it.

U.S. Naval ATSB, Hiệp Hòa Sugar Mill, the "Brown Water Navy"

Located on the Vàm Cỏ Đông River northwest of Saigon, Hiệp Hòa Sugar Mill served as an ATSB for American naval forces. PBR (Patrol Boat\River) units patrolled the sector of river around the site as part of the Operation GIANT SLINGSHOT anti-infiltration campaign. The river forces disrupted the constant flow of communist men and munitions into the capital region. While the river sailors used the sugar mill for sleeping quarters, the Seabees began construction of better quarters, base defense, fuel and ammunition storage, and a helicopter pad.

The Naval Support Activities (NSA) was the infrastructure that supported the naval warfare effort in Vietnam. Whether the NSA was a shore installation or a floating barge complex, the support activities were the home base for all the logistics that kept the boats and aircraft operational. Without their efforts, the operations of the ships, boats, and aircraft of the Brown Water Navy could not have been sustained.

My technical problem might have been difficult but seemed well defined. To the contrary, the sabotage challenge by the communists was a tougher problem and much more complex. I contacted Vice Admiral Chung Tấn Cang, head of the Vietnamese Navy, asking for the protection of my fluvial convoy from the port of Saigon to the mill site. The director of the Saigon port, Nguyễn văn Chiểu, supplied a huge 60-ton crane and his biggest barge with 16 independent compartments. In case the communists hit the barge, there were still many compartments left to keep the barge afloat. On both sides of the river, I asked the local district chiefs to provide local militia to ambush the VC along the way to Hiệp Hòa to avoid bazooka attacks. Each piece of equipment on the barge had a float attached to it by nylon ropes. In case of sinking, the crane was able to retrieve the sunken parts. Of course, the convoy was preceded by mine sweepers. High speed gun boats patrolled both sides of the river to prevent enemy attacks. In the air, I asked for the report of enemy movement by a small observation aircraft. Last but not least, I promised to the soldiers a victory celebration when the equipment arrived safe at the mill. It was a known fact that Hiệp Hòa Sugar Mill produced the best rum in Vietnam from its by-product molasses. It was really a very unique and challenging project in my career. Thank God, the convoy full of equipment arrived at the mill safely. It was one of my "trophies" of the war time effort. The soldiers and the mill staff did really celebrate that important milestone day.

The sugar mill grinding season lasted about 6 months every year. After the grinding season, the staff kept working on repairs and maintenance and/or modernization work to get ready for the next crop of cane. The year 1963 was exceptional with the total replacement of very old equipment. My next critical milestones were the completion of the foundation, the equipment installation and finally the trial run of the mill.

I did not realize that I was walking into a really explosive minefield of political, technical, financial and life-threatening challenges. My own life was exposed to serious communist threat because the communist policy was to sabotage and destroy any government industrial plant to create shortage of goods and stop any economic development. If the sugar mill could be stopped then thousands of cane farmers would lose their jobs and this type of unemployment would be exploited by the communists. They wanted to bring chaos to the economy. From this new job, I learned that the security challenge to an engineer during war time was much more difficult than the tough technical problems facing him.

I had another political problem. Most of the French trained engineers preferred to work among their counterparts. In 1958, I happened to be the very first generation of Vietnamese trained in America and working in Saigon. It was sad that such rivalry between French and American trained groups existed in the old French colony. I felt isolated in my daily task. There was an unwritten rule that Vietnamese who had graduated from Paris' "Grandes Écoles" would dominate the Saigon administration. To be the first MIT trained engineer working with this group was no easy task. I had to work with the staff of Hiệp Hòa sugar mill and the Khánh Hội refinery near the port of Saigon. All of the executive staff was from French universities and the Vice Chairman of the board of Directors, Mr. Polton, from the famous École Polytechnique in Paris. With this background of rivalry, I was very careful in my decision-making process to avoid any technical minefield. The positive side of this competitiveness: it made me a better engineer.

View of the mill site

This aerial view above shows the Hiệp Hòa Sugar Mill with white rectangular roof in the center of the photo. It was located on the North side of the Vàm Cỏ (Waico) River. The dark green zone with trees near the mill was the workers housing quarters. The straight-line canal next to it and the wide gray horizontal Vàm Cỏ (Waico) River were the "freeways" of Vietnam. Waterways were needed for low cost barge transportation of sugar cane from the plantations to the mill. The annual harvest from November to May was about 400,000 tons of cane yielding about 40,000 tons of brown, unrefined sugar. Thousand of hectares of cane plantation surrounded the mill.

This area was only about 10 miles from the Cambodian border infested with communist insurgents.

Modern steam turbine replacing old steam reciprocating engine with huge flywheel

Mill driven by steam turbines and gear boxes

Sugar cane being fed to the mill

Vàm Cỏ River near Hiệp Hòa Sugar Mill. Villages were infiltrated by VC in 1960

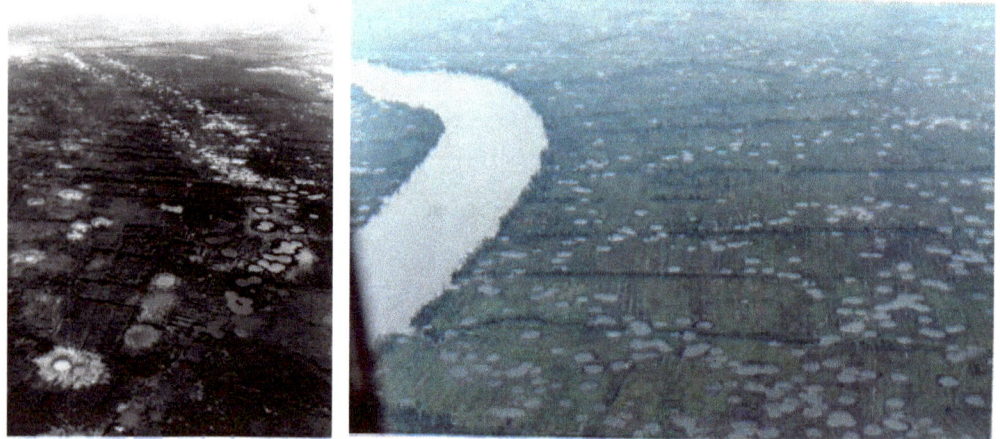
Vàm Cỏ Tây River near Hiệp Hòa Sugar Mill, an area pockmarked by B-52 bomb craters

A bomb explosion near the mill

A typical supply convoy from the port of Saigon to the mill escorted by the Armed Forces

Typical Sugar Cane Plantation at Hiệp-Hòa

The cane grows to about 8–10 ft tall. My Cessna plane was hit from this typical field

Zigzagging Vàm Cỏ River from Saigon to Hiệp-Hòa Sugar Mill

As stated, the heavy equipment of the mill could be transported only by barges on the Vàm Cỏ River because existing bridges from the Saigon Port to Hiệp Hòa could not take the heavy loads. This alone gave the VC a very good opportunity to sink the barges by Bazooka or rockets from the two sides of the river. They could also mine the river near the villages controlled by them at night. I was facing huge security problems daily. With the declassified documents of the CIA, it is clear now that the communist National Liberation Front had its headquarters in Cambodia on the opposite side of the Hiệp Hòa Sugar Mill Waico River. The VC was protected by the Cambodian government.

As Technical Director of the company, I had to make many business field trips from the Saigon head office to the factory. Each time I felt my life was in real danger.

US Navy river patrol boat protecting Hiệp Hòa Sugar Mill

U.S. Naval ATSB [Advanced Tactical Support Base] protecting Hiệp Hòa Sugar Mill

(Extract from US ARMY NEWS: October 1963)

The following information from the US Army gave a clear picture of what was going on in this "hot" zone.

HIỆP HÒA

"……*The area development programs soon evolved into combat operations, and by the end of October 1963, the network also had responsibility for [Cambodian] border surveillance...*"

"*...The Hiệp Hòa Special Forces Camp was strategically situated just north of Highway TL7A and east of the Sông Vàm Cỏ Đông River in the densely populated and hotly contested Plain of Reeds located approximately 22 miles west-northwest of Saigon and 24 miles south-southeast of Tây Ninh. It was also 11 miles east of the South Vietnamese/Cambodian border and Cambodia's infamous "Parrot's Beak," which was a major Viet Cong (VC) staging area. The 125 by 100 meter camp was built on the bank of a canal encircled with barbed wire. It was protected by .30-caliber machinegun emplacements on all four corners and two 81mm mortars located near the front gates. Surrounding the camp were numerous villages, sugar cane plantations and rice fields...*"

"*...HIỆP HÒA - Since moving to the Hiệp Hòa area near the Sugar Mill, the combined forces of the 2nd Battalion, 27th Infantry, Wolfhounds, reconnaissance platoon and their Popular Forces counterparts have been a real thorn in the sides of the enemy in his efforts to move supplies and personnel from staging areas inside Cambodia. In recent activity southwest of Fire Support Base Dixon, the forces combined to kill four NVA and uncover a small cache they apparently were guarding. Acting on intelligence reports that seven NVA were in the area, the allies began just south of FSB Dixon to search for the enemy. "We hadn't gone very far when our point man spotted two people disappearing into a hole," recalled First Lieutenant Robert Barclay of Chamblee, Ga. "As we were advancing toward their position one of them tossed a grenade out of the hole." I yelled 'grenade' and everyone got down. Luckily it failed to go off. While my men were keeping them pinned down with small arms fire, I crawled up and dropped a grenade in the hole." Along with two bodies there were two AK-47s, one B-40 rocket launcher and six rockets, one Chicom grenade, some AK rounds and some food discovered. After a break for chow the men again moved out this time spotting a small air hole in the ground. "After we spotted the air hole we threw a smoke grenade in to see if there was another opening," explained First Lieutenant Mark Davis from San Antonio, Tex. "When we saw the smoke coming from another small hole, we began moving towards it when two NVA popped up and opened up with their AK's." As before, the enemy was silenced by a grenade. This time two AK's and small arms ammunition and magazines were discovered...*"

Perils of Industrialization during War Time

In 1963, Mr. Trương văn Tố, Chairman of the Board, and I made a trip to the mills to see the latest progress of the construction phase of the modernization project. We had a French sedan Peugeot 403. We were almost certain that the VC would try to kill us for newspaper headlines and political gain. Our safety plan was to stop at the office of Đức Hòa town's Mayor, a colonel, to ask for military protection for the dangerous part of the road. The Mayor organized an escort with a disguised civilian passenger bus full of well armed soldiers. When we left town, the red laterite road was dug up at several places overnight by the VC. A bad sign! Traffic was required to slow down to about 5 MPH. At one turn of the road, suddenly three black pajamas peasants, about 20 ft away from us, stood up from the cane field and opened fire at us. Thank God, they missed and immediately the soldiers from the escort bus returned the fire and killed all the three communist insurgents. I was all shook-up because I really felt so close to death. It was the first time in my life that I had eye-witnessed human killing at close range. I did join the soldiers to inspect the three black pajamas corpses. We found photos of Ho Chi Minh, their own families and communist propaganda documents in their pockets.

Photo showing a soldier checking ID of a farmer in black pajama

The problem was any farmer could be a disguised communist. Our small convoy continued safely to the mill. I remembered feeling very scared on the return trip via the same road because of possible revenge. After this deadly ambush, I decided to build an

800 meters long airstrip next to the mill for the use of our staff. The runway was made of compacted laterite. All supervisory staff was required to travel by air to avoid kidnapping. Air Vietnam used the four seat Cessna propeller plane for the shuttle service. On each payroll day, the head office simply dropped a bag full of cash to avoid ambush on the road.

Vàm Cỏ Đông River, near the mill,
a site where locals used community fishing to disguise resupply of VC

Vàm Cỏ Tây River at Hiệp Hòa

This seemingly peaceful area was full of deadly ambushes from both sides of the river

Typical Sugar Cane wooden junk en route to Hiệp Hòa Sugar Mill via the Vàm Cỏ River

After three years with the Vietnam Sugar Company, what did I learn?

The management of a project during wartime almost cost my life two times, one in the air and the other on the road. My success depended so much on the cooperation of the armed forces and too many obstacles were way above my control. I had the good luck to have met new good friends for life. They helped me in the field of electrical engineering because I knew only the mechanical side. Mr. Hồ Tấn Phát, alumnus of Supélec, Paris Grande École, CEO of Vietnam Power Company and his talented team member Mr. Nguyễn văn Dậu, both solved all the electrical problems for me. One of the best rewards was to have all the French trained engineers in the sugar company becoming my friends for life although there was rivalry at the beginning. The success depended so much on human relations and team work.

My experience at the Hiệp Hòa Sugar Company was a wake-up call for me to see the complexity and magnitude of the enormous challenges that South Vietnam was facing in the industrial sector in the midst of a raging war. I was then able to understand that the comfortable and carefree life I had with the large American corporation Esso was rather a superficial existence for a well-trained professional like me when my country was plunged into a fierce armed conflict. That was the reason for me to leave the Hiệp Hòa Sugar Company and join government service to be more useful to my country with the professional technical knowledge I had acquired from MIT. I did totally give the best of myself in the following ten years to serve successively as Director of the Government Industrial Development Center, President of the Industrial Development Bank and Deputy Minister of Economy in charge of Commerce and Industry. My story "EAST meets WEST" goes on in South Vietnam mixed with the horrors of war before it reaches the peaceful Golden State in the USA.

CHAPTER 13

Offshore Oil Exploration

Vietnam's Great Potential for Off-Shore Oil & Gas Development!

The cover of Management Magazine Oct. 1974

Mr. Trần Văn Khởi, the engineer who served as Head of the Vietnam Agency for Petroleum and Minerals, published the book entitled "DẦU HỎA VIỆT NAM 1970-1975," which describes Vietnam's oil and gas exploration during that period.

1966: THE VERY BEGINNING OF VIETNAM'S OFF-SHORE OIL & GAS DEVELOPMENT

During war time, the discovery of oil in Vietnam was a great event for the war effort. In 1966, the CCOP ("Coordinating Committee for Offshore Prospecting in Asia") was initiated by China, Japan, Republic of Korea and The Philippines under the auspices of ESCAP (Economic and Social Commission for Asia and the Pacific) and the United Nations. CCOP became an independent intergovernmental organization in 1987 based on the common understanding of its member countries and the aspirations of the United Nations. The name was changed in 1994, but the acronym CCOP was retained. CCOP has devoted itself to the co-ordination of, and co-operation in, scientific activities related to coastal and offshore areas with respect to geological/geophysical surveys, regional map compilations, database development, development of human resources and transfer of state of the art technology.

The very beginning of Vietnam Offshore Oil began in 1968. While working at the Ministry of Economy, I coordinated with CCOP in Bangkok to welcome a very important technical assistance mission to Vietnam. CCOP sent a high-tech team of three specialists from London Imperial College to Saigon to help the Vietnam Off-Shore Exploration Project. Vietnam was a CCOP member while Great Britain, Germany, and Holland provided financial and technical contributions to this organization. Its initial report on Vietnam oil potential was not optimistic.

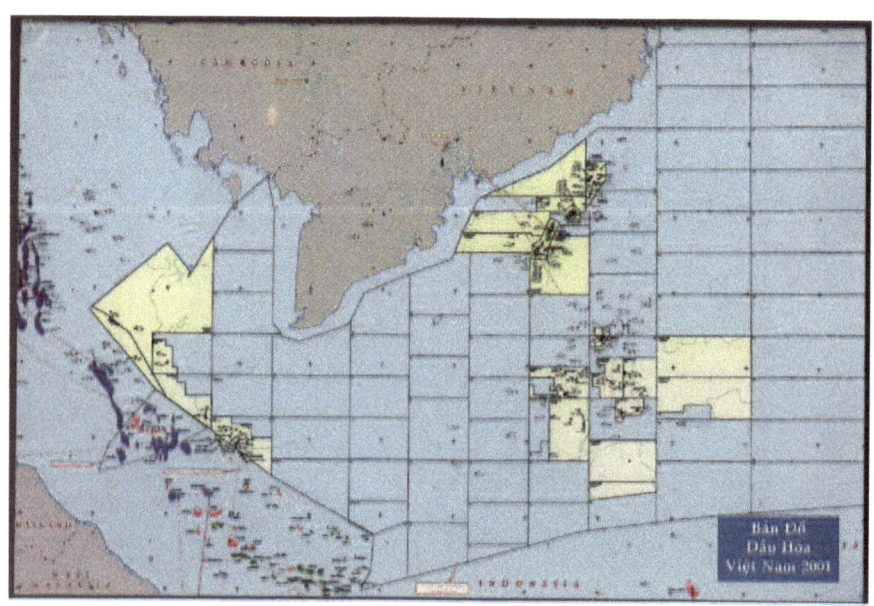

Map of Vietnam Offshore oil fields 2001

Offshore Oil Exploration

In 1968, we set up the headquarters of this international team at Saigon's famous Majestic Hotel, on Tự Do Street. They needed 10,000 kg of explosives and two ocean going ships for the two month seismic survey of the continental shelf off Vietnam. I explained the importance of this project, and the technical requirements of this international team to Rear Admiral Trần văn Chơn, the head of the Vietnamese Navy. Obviously, during this critical phase of the war, the discovery of oil and gas in the country was important, and indeed critical for the survival of Vietnam's war time economy. Because of this I received full cooperation from the Armed Forces.

I was assigned the responsibility of coordinating the transportation of explosives to the Navy ships with the military staff of Thành Thủy Hạ Ammunition Depot located in the suburb of Saigon. A convoy of trucks from this depot through downtown Saigon, then to the ships was extremely dangerous and complicated because of obvious sabotage efforts by the Communists. The MP (Military Police) escort for the explosives to the Embarcadero proceeded without incident. To celebrate this important milestone day for the Vietnam economy, Admiral Chơn invited me to join him in the ceremonial sendoff party with Navy band and honor guards at the Saigon River pier. We were all very proud and fortunate to be the first Vietnamese team participating in the exploration of Vietnam's offshore oil and gas. As a goodwill gesture, I did not forget to put two cases of Johnny Walker Black Label on the ships for the team's two month expedition at sea.

I was told by the petroleum specialists that the experts could detonate 200 kg of explosives at a time on the Navy warships, as opposed to 100 kg that could be detonated ordinarily on civilian ships, because of the difference in the thickness of the steel hulls. As a result, the reflection and refraction waves through the sediment and rocks were better recorded for the study of the continental shelf. The good news was that, according to the findings, the Saigon Sabu basin sediments were similar to those on the other side of the continent. The rocks and the sea floor vegetation were the same. This was good news because production of oil and gas on the Sabu (Malaysia) side had already begun many years before.

During one of the dinner banquets at the Majestic Hotel, I sat next to the Director of the Massachusetts Wood Hole Oceanographic Institute. He was a member of ECAFE (The United Nations Economic Commission for Asia and the Far East) team with a lot of experience in the exploration phase. I asked him about the crude oil potential of the Saigon Sabu Basin, Vietnam side. At first he refused to give me a guesstimate. I kept insisting and promised not to leak any news concerning his estimate. Finally he uttered 10 billion barrels based on what he saw in the similar structure from the Borneo Sabu side. He kept warning me not to leak any numbers to the hungry press. I felt so happy to hear this news. I thought "My God, it's quite a revelation; and so critical to the survival of the Vietnamese war economy! Maybe with this newly found wealth, the US will not let the communists take over all that oil! And maybe the US Congress may reconsider its drastic aid cutting and let Vietnam survive a few more years." It was wishful thinking!

The critical issue was that several years were needed for the production platform to be constructed and prepare for the exploration phase to transition to the exploitation phase. Sadly, we knew that the US Congress had cut the Vietnam war budget against the wishes of the Executive branch in the White House for continued aid.

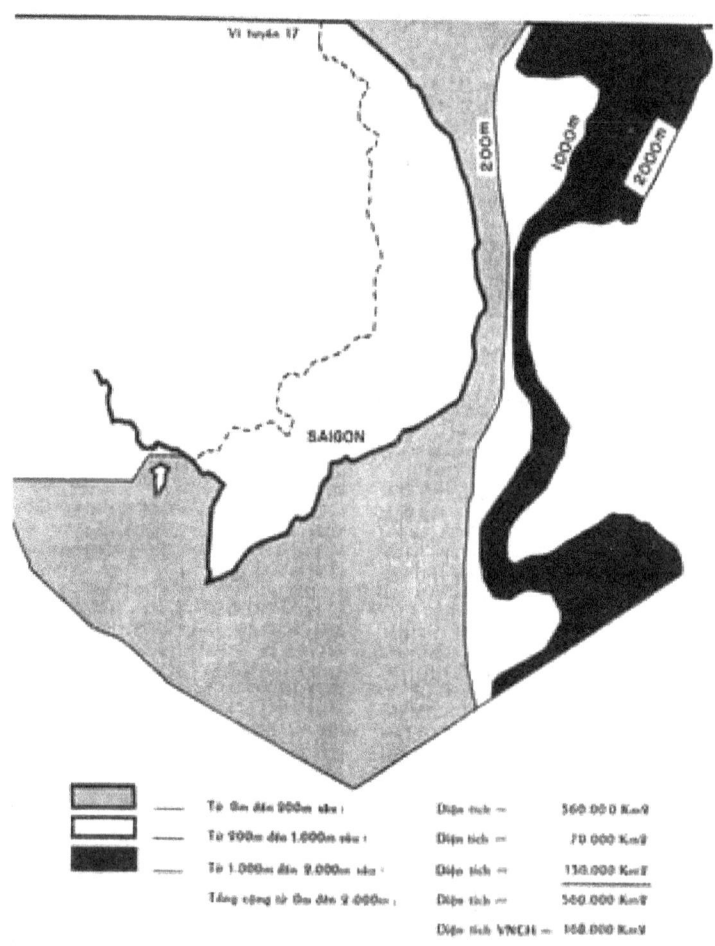

Depth of the Continental Shelf of Vietnam in meters

Offshore Oil Exploration

Visit to Vietnam Shell Oil Drilling Platform 1974
Left to Right:
Mr. Hồ Tấn Phát, President of Viet Nam Power Company, Mr. Trần văn Khởi, CEO Petroleum and Minerals Agency - Republic of China's Ambassador to Viet Nam, HE Nguyễn văn Kiểu, Viet Nam Ambassador to the Republic of China, Mr. Khương Hữu Điểu, President of Industrial Development Bank, Shell Drilling Specialist - Sikorsky Helicopter in the background

Management Magazine 10-1974
Petroleum Prospects and Economic Development in Vietnam By KHƯƠNG HỮU ĐIỂU

Vietnam's First Oil Drilling Operation
Time: 14:10, 8.17.1974 Ocean-Prospector Platform

Management Magazine 10-1974
Oil & Gas in Vietnam

Offshore Oil Exploration

Offshore oil was discovered in 1974. At that time, I felt very proud to have a bottle of Vietnam sweet base crude oil in my office, a symbol of hope for our economy. During the war, I was the chairman of the joint Vietnam-Shell-Esso refinery. We rejected the Quảng Ngãi site for many obvious economic reasons. Furthermore, we could not build a refinery during the war because a US$ 1000 rocket could burn down the oil refinery - a multi-billion dollar investment.

Sadly, my dream and hope to see a prosperous South Vietnam ultimately did not come true. By April 1975, it turned into a nightmare because of the Vietnam "Bolshevik Revolution."

In 2010 Kissinger, for the first time in a State Department conference, told the audience that the loss of the war was not because the South Vietnamese Army did not fight, but because the US decided to change its policy toward the communists. To open the door to Communist China was more important to the US foreign policy than to fight the North Vietnamese communists. It was observed that the more the US isolated Red China, the stronger Mao Tse Tung became. Vietnam, a small country, was once more, the hopeless and convenient pawn of the Great Powers chess game.

After 1975, Communist Vietnam no longer had to deal with the pre-war security problem. Feasibility studies showed situating the refinery at Dung Quất was contrary to all economic criteria. There was no commercial port. The port of Dung Quất had many other major problems. It is not large enough nor was it well equipped enough to allow the unloading of the heavy equipment for the refinery. The road from the port to the refinery site was also in poor condition.

The Communists took 34 long years to build the first oil refinery in Vietnam. Worst of all, it was built at the wrong place with the wrong capacity. Why? Again, Communist politics.

It was a well-known fact around the world that the Vietnamese government would grant approval for an oil refinery based only on specific political reasons. It had to be built in the central Quảng Ngãi region of Vietnam because their communist leader Phạm văn Đồng was born there. In 1930, he was a charter member of the Indochinese Communist party, and he served as Prime Minister of the Socialist Republic of Vietnam for three decades.

As it turned out, the refinery project was finally slated to begin in the 1980's. At first, it was supposed to be constructed near the port of Vũng Tàu, just 100 km (60 mi) away from the offshore oil fields. However, the refinery project was shelved. Why? In the early 1990s, Total SA (France) expressed interest in the project. At the same time, the Vietnamese government decided to move the site to Dung Quất. Following this, in

1995 Total SA pulled out, claiming that the new site made no economic sense. Total SA was replaced with a consortium of foreign investors, including the LG Group and Petronas, but this consortium also withdrew two years later citing the same economic reasons.

In 1998, Viet Ross, a joint venture of Vietnam and Russia, was established. The intergovernmental agreement on the construction and operation of the refinery was signed on 25 August 1998. The Front End Engineering Design (FEED) contract was signed between Petro Vietnam, Zarubezhneft and Foster Wheeler Energy. Construction of the Dung Quất refinery was originally scheduled to begin in 2000, but the process was delayed several times. On December 25th, 2002, Russia pulled out for the same economic reasons, and the project continued under the management of Petrovietnam, a state enterprise. Finally, the refinery was inaugurated on February 25th, 2009, *34 years* after the war. The long delay and the political decision to build at the wrong site caused great long term financial loss for the country, and consequently the construction costs increased from $1.3 billion to $3 billion dollars.

For a period of more than 30 years, Communist Vietnam kept exporting crude oil and importing costly refined products such as diesel oil and gasoline for their own use. The leaders recognized the need to have an oil refinery to sustain the country's economic development but were incapable of building one.

The Dung Quất refinery was 1000 km from the country's Bạch Hổ (White Tiger) oil field off the Southern coast. This would increase the cost of transportation of crude oil and refined products. They would probably need to construct an additional pipeline to solve this long-term logistics problem. The site was also situated far from the country's economic centers, Saigon and Hanoi. Of the refined crude oil, 60% would be shipped back to Saigon, 30% to Hanoi, and only 10% would be used locally.

Not until 2011 did communist Vietnam via Petro Vietnam admit that it had learned a lesson from its first oil refinery. The chairman of PetroVietnam was quoted as saying that future facilities should be built according to sound economic feasibility studies.

Investing in future refineries with such a wrong capacity would be inefficient. The state Vietnam News quoted Đinh La Thăng, chairman of PetroVietnam, as saying: "This is the lesson drawn from Dung Quất." Thăng also added that there was a plan to build two refineries located in North and South Vietnam with an annual capacity of 10 million tons of oil each. PetroVietnam confirmed his comments with AFP.

Offshore Oil Exploration

Location of new refineries in North and South Vietnam

Dung Quất Refinery

END OF VOLUME 1

www.ingramcontent.com/pod-product-compliance
Lightning Source LLC
Chambersburg PA
CBHW061109070526
44583CB00027B/3238